Thrown Away Children:
Sky's Story

Thrown Away Children: Sky's Story

By Louise Allen
with Theresa McEvoy

WELBECK

Published by Welbeck
An imprint of Welbeck Non-Fiction Limited,
part of Welbeck Publishing Group.
Based in London and Sydney.

First published by Welbeck in 2022

ISBN
Paperback – 9781802790788
UK eBook – 9781802790795
US eBook – 9781802794083

Typeset by Roger Walker
Printed in Great Britain by CPI Books, Chatham, Kent

10 9 8 7 6 5 4 3

The Forest Stewardship Council® is an international
nongovernmental organisation that promotes environmentally
appropriate, socially beneficial, and economically viable management
of the world's forests. To learn more, visit www.fsc.org

www.welbeckpublishing.com

*For all the children young and grown
who have experienced abuse
and neglect.*

Foreword

Sky's story is one of the most extreme and challenging of the fostering situations I have ever experienced.

I was disturbed by this child much more than the others, and it has taken me a long time to figure out why. I think it was so frightening because it was a reminder that I had fallen into the trap of thinking I 'knew' about people and life, and the experience with Sky – and her mother – utterly destroyed that certainty.

Like everyone else, I am learning every day, and the more I *think* I know, the more I discover that I am actually *sure* about less and less.

We had no idea who and what we were letting through the front door.

PART ONE:
Before

I. Denise

'You're not helping!'

Denise feels personally affronted by the inconsiderate position of the pavement.

Lethargic, low-spirited, and more than a little resentful that a big fat bucket of trouble has dropped into her lap on a Friday afternoon, she needs three attempts to reverse her Vauxhall Corsa in between two parked cars. This does nothing to improve her mood. She suspects that all the shunting backwards and forwards, and the disturbing little noises she heard as she stuffed up the manoeuvre, mean that she will have scraped the wheels and rims along the kerb. Not for the first time today, she curses the name 'Wiseman/ Hopfgarten' that appears on the front of the new and fairly useless file sitting on the passenger seat.

This shouldn't really be her case anyway: her load is full. More than full. Her team leader, Philip, knows that and has dumped it on her anyway. Plus, it has come from nowhere, so there's no background to go on. There isn't even actual confirmation of children living at the address, let alone names and ages. She hates turning up unannounced at the front door, but no one has answered the calls she has put in at regular intervals since lunchtime when the complaint first came in. It will be nothing, of course. Nosy neighbours interfering because they've fallen out over something, and this is a good way to get back at someone. But the allegation is serious enough that Philip insisted they investigate immediately, before the end of the day, before the weekend.

Denise slams the car door shut, hitches her trousers up at the waist where they have slipped down during the drive, and clicks at the button on the key fob to lock it.

It is as she turns towards the house that the smell first hits her.

The stench is putrid, toxic and utterly overwhelming. Almost involuntarily, she puts her hand to her face to block her nose and cover her mouth. In spite of that, she still gags a little as she steps forward. There must be a good 20 feet to go until she reaches the front door, and she wonders how she will make it without some sort of protective mask. Denise feels no need to double-check her notes for the house number. She has no doubt whatsoever that she is in the right place. She holds her breath as she takes another step forward.

She has been so busy concentrating on managing her parking manoeuvre that she hasn't really registered the environment. Only now does she scan the area in front of the house and begin to take in the mess of a garden. 'Garden' is about as far removed as it is possible to be from the chaotic space in front of her. There is no grass, or flowers, or shrubs. Instead, abandoned white goods are balanced at seemingly precarious angles amidst overflowing bin liners, a horribly stained mattress, tyres, chairs, paint pots, broken flowerpots, a length of drainpipe and a rotting roll of carpet.

Denise wonders how it is possible to have got through that many fridges in a lifetime – or perhaps some of them are freezers. Even so. It's like staring into one of the containers at the amenity tip, though the local council does a far better job of organising the rubbish there. It must be

4

where the smell is coming from, the collective decay of this decomposing dump.

Mercifully, the path to the front door is relatively clear, though debris is piled high on either side.

The stench intensifies with each step that Denise takes.

When she knocks on the door, the strangest thing happens.

II. Hanna

Denise doesn't know that she is being carefully observed from inside the house.

Hanna has anticipated the visit and has been listening out for the sound of the car. Not answering the phone will only ever work for a finite amount of time, she knows, and it has rung a lot today.

But this lot will always step up their attacks – which means putting other preventative measures into action. This is an arena in which Hanna is uniquely skilful.

Oh yes.

Hanna leans forward and pulls back a tattered curtain a fraction from the window. She watches the woman attempt to parallel park, incompetently, and emerge from the car. She sees a young woman, probably a similar age to herself, late twenties, perhaps early thirties, conservatively dressed; the woman's outfit is attempting to be smart-casual rather than too businesslike, but you can always tell. Beige trouser suit, neutral tones. Mid-height heels. Average height and build, no obvious distinguishing features. Here's a woman trapped in between the opposing constructs of beauty as defined by the male gaze, and a sort of corporate comfort.

Stupid.

They might be a similar age, but very different life experiences mean that they don't even look like the same species. And it goes way beyond dress sense.

Bitch probably won't even have children of her own, so what can she know?

Hanna tuts aloud.

She almost feels sorry for the social worker. Almost, but not quite. They are on different sides, after all. And that bag is certainly big enough to contain a folder or clipboard full of paperwork lies.

So Hanna isn't taking any chances.

She beetles her way through the debris piled in the narrow hallway. She knows exactly where to step, sure-footed as a mountain goat in an environment that she has constructed. Clearing the corridor of obstacles has never occurred to her as an idea. Housework is a bourgeois binary construct which Hanna rejects. Time spent cleaning means time away from her political work, a sacrifice that Hanna is not prepared to make. Besides satisfying the hoarding tendencies, the barricade of newspapers and household items also acts as a defence mechanism against unwanted intruders like this one. Keeping people like this out of her home has become more than a game to Hanna. Protection of one's home is a political right, not a privilege.

The rap comes so half-heartedly on the metal letter box that Hanna knows this woman is already beaten. She stifles a delighted laugh. She could chew this one up and spit her out: she is not even able to bang on a door with any kind of authority.

Still, she sends the precautionary text upstairs:

DEVICES OFF. NO SOUNDS. BACK AWAY FROM WINDOWS.

Predictive text picks up the well-worn words. It is a familiar message; all know the drill and the part each must play. Hanna waits until she hears the click of an upstairs

7

bedroom door closing before she allows the front door to open a crack.

Hanna imagines how unsettling this must be for Beige Trousers on the other side of the door in her heels-but-not-really-heels corporate costume.

'Hello?'

The voice from outside is as tentative as the pathetic knock. If this was a boxing match, the referee would be stepping in to end it. Hanna decides to let her stew for a bit longer and makes no reply, leaving Beige Trousers to make the next move.

'Um, Mrs… Wiseman? May I come in?'

'Not my name. But state yours, and your purpose.'

Beige Trousers is clearly taken aback. Through the crack Hanna sees her take a step away from the door.

That's right. Back off, bitch.

'Um, apologies. I'm Denise Carlson, from the social services team? Mrs… Hopfgarten. We'd like to help you?'

Hanna is unable to keep the sneer from her voice at the inadequacy of someone making declarative statements sound like questions. 'The best way to help me would be to turn around, walk back the way you came, and exit my property.'

Hanna feels the slightest of pushes against the front door, as though this Denise Carlson person is testing it.

Got you, bitch.

Hanna's hand whips around the door frame, recording already in progress on the phone. Her voice is clear and assured as she provides the commentary.

'Social worker attempting forced entry at our property. 4.50pm, Friday 10 February. Has already been asked to leave once. Now pushing directly against the front door

8

in order to gain access. We are not free, even inside our own homes!'

Hanna's voice rises passionately in the final statement. She is on a roll now.

'Perpetrator has identified herself voluntarily as Denise Carlson. She is female, in her late twenties, possibly early thirties...'

Hanna can't quite see from this angle, but it appears as if Beige Trousers is trying to cover her face. This will make excellent footage when she uploads it later.

Hanna's voice rises again as she begins to get carried away. 'It is my life and my choice how to live it. You have no right, and the state has no right, to bring down judgement on innocent citizens due to ignorant subscription to hegemonic beliefs.'

There is the clack-clack sound of Beige Trousers' half-heels retreating on the pebbled path.

'And she is now exiting the premises,' Hanna finishes with a triumphant flourish.

She slams the door, satisfied with a job well done. 'And fuck the hell off,' she says under her breath, recording concluded. In spite of the coarseness of the words, her accent is finest cut-glass English, barely a trace of the European heritage she hides. She rues briefly, as she does often, the day she first set foot in this godforsaken country that has claimed her, body and soul.

It is a victory today, but Hanna knows that there will be more battles to come. These people don't give up. And she will be ready when the next offensive is launched.

She keys into her phone: *Well done, my darlings. We are safe once more.*

Steps thud overhead when the message is delivered and a shadow, wider than it is tall, appears at the top of the stairs.

'KFC to celebrate, my darling?'

Busy congratulating herself, Hanna doesn't hear Denise talking into her mobile phone outside, urging her supervisor to request an EPO – an Emergency Protection Order.

III. Denise

'Of course I *know* it's a serious step. I've never requested one before precisely because—'

Philip cuts her off at the other end. 'The court are going to have to be satisfied that the EPO is necessary and proportionate and that there is no less radical form of order available.'

'Don't quote the rulebook at me. I know all this, but—'

'So Denise-Denise?' He repeats her name in the sing-song voice of the Randy & The Rainbows' song. 'You're telling me that you haven't even been inside?'

'No, I haven't even seen past the front door, but—'

'And so we don't actually know if there are children living permanently at the address?'

'No. I mean I've read the whole file but to be honest, there isn't much there. I haven't been able to investigate much more. You only gave it to me this afternoon, remember?'

'So it could be that a child visits and isn't resident. We don't want to be too heavy-handed here, right?'

'Look, even so, it's all really unsettling. The place is like nothing you've ever seen. And what's just happened to me with the filming, well, that's just odd.'

'Oh, we all get filmed, darling. You must just be looking particularly photogenic today.'

Denise knows Philip well enough not to be put off by his light-hearted tone. He is her supervisor, he has a wealth of experience and he's one of the best. She wants to make sure that he has got the message.

'Not like this. There was something so—' she isn't quite sure of the word she wants. 'Calculated. Trust me on this?'

Her words still come out with the up-lilt of a question, even though Denise is more sure than she has ever been before that if there is a child in that house, then he or she needs to get out. 'We can claim that Section 47 Enquiries are being frustrated by unreasonable refusal of access to a child, and we have more than reasonable cause to believe that access is needed as a matter of urgency.'

'Oh, Denise, dooby doo. It's a good job I'm so in love with you.'

'I'm not sure what Matt would think about that, but thank you. Set the wheels in motion here, Philip. Do something. Come back and visit with me if you like. Honestly, this is the weirdest thing I've ever seen.'

It's more than just the smell and the aggressive behaviour of the woman behind the door with her camera, her strange language choices that make the suburb of Crickleborough sound like some sort of police state, and the disgusting mess of a front garden – though they are compelling factors on their own.

No, it is a prickling, tingling sensation that she can't quite explain. A sixth sense about how wrong things are behind that door.

Denise spends the evening poring over the scant case notes. The thing that ruined her Friday afternoon, and that she initially wanted nothing to do with, has got right under her skin. Partly it's because it's so difficult to understand how things have got to this stage. God only knows where that footage has ended up – Denise has googled various keywords, praying that she won't actually find it and that it was just an idle threat from Hanna. The bizarre filming treatment is apparently commonplace – a tactic that Hanna has used before. Representatives from the housing association were the first people to contact social services when their attempts to make contact with the family were either ignored, or the door was partly opened and Hanna's arm would appear with a mobile phone in her hand, recording the event.

Know how you feel, thinks Denise, ruefully.

The saga seems to have been going on for several years, though it has only recently been passed to social services because no one knew, at least for a good while, that there was a child involved. There are lots of photocopies of originals, lots of notes, and some of the paperwork isn't chronological, or even clear enough to read in places. What Denise manages to piece together is this:

Neighbours complained to the housing association of the dirt and mess created by the family. There are a number of reports of this nature, and Denise is frankly surprised that there aren't more. So it began as a council issue, nothing to do with her department.

Then there are records of a couple of phone calls, again from neighbours, suggesting that a child was going in and out of the house.

Local shopkeepers reported to the police their concern that a young girl was shoplifting and behaving strangely, and there is a suggestion, unconfirmed, that she is linked with the Crickleborough address that Denise attended this afternoon.

Yet nothing very much seems to have been done about any of this, as far as Denise can tell. How have this family escaped detection for so long?

Because they are not the average family, the voice in her head grimly tells her.

She reads on.

The clincher, and the reason that Philip has saddled Denise with the case, is the result of dogged, determined action from a local primary school – and from one woman in particular. Crickleborough Primary welcomed a new head teacher two years ago, a young woman named Rowena Edmund. Denise knows the school; she already has connections there through her caseload, though not directly with this head teacher. But she knows how much they struggle to get children to attend and families to engage, given that the school is situated within such a low socio-economic catchment area. This Miss Edmund seems to have made it a key priority to improve attendance as part of her mission to turn the school around.

There are copies of a number of letters. There appears to have been quite a bit of correspondence with this head teacher, who has also been doing a bit of independent investigation – some of the legwork that should have been taken up by social services, Denise is ashamed to admit to herself. There are several pages of statements and background information that she has compiled. Rowena Edmund is nothing if not persistent. After liaising with the Education Welfare Officer for the catchment secondary school, who has attempted to visit on several occasions, the head teacher reported her findings to the children's services. Denise checks the date: nearly a month ago. Crikey.

And it might have waited even longer, she realises. It was only after another telephone call raising concerns about a child at the address had also come into the child protection team that afternoon, from a member of the public, that

Philip had finally made the connection and sent Denise round there.

Then Denise reads something that makes her do a double take.

Oh God.

Why didn't she spot that this afternoon before she made the visit?

'Well, thanks for *that*, buddy,' Denise says, sucking her teeth. The buddy in question is Philip, even though he isn't in her sitting room and definitely can't hear her. He's probably miles away, in fact, no doubt enjoying a night out with his partner, Matt.

Denise tops up her wine glass and reaches for her phone. Though it is always difficult to stop thinking about work in her job, where she regularly sees humankind at its most abusive, and it is often difficult to get the plight of individuals out of her head, she never usually takes work home with her like this. She is, she decides, going to make an exception in this case.

'It's Friday night,' Philip says.

The faux-stern tone doesn't fool Denise. 'Well, hello to you, too. What sort of a greeting is that? I'm well aware it's Friday night, thank you.'

'Then this is a social call?'

'Not exactly, though it does relate to social work.'

'If it's not a social call then you shouldn't be calling your boss at all. Work is over for today, Denise-Denise, and the cocktail hour is starting.'

'Except that it's not.'

'It most certainly is. Cosmopolitans tonight. I do like a pink drink, as you know. Matt's already pouring. And doing his best Tom Cruise bartender impression to go with it.'

'I mean, work isn't over.'

'I've said yes to your emergency application, haven't I? Knock, knock.'

'I haven't got time for jokes, Philip.'

'Lighten up. Knock, knock.'

'Who's there?'

'Interrupting cow.'

'Interrupting cow—'

Before Denise can get the 'who' out at the end of the response, Philip is bellowing 'Moooo!' down the phone at her. She can hear the giggles and snorts of laughter at the other end.

'Not funny, Philip. Are you suggesting I'm an interrupting cow, now?'

'Of course I'm not. It's just a funny joke.'

'If you're five years old.'

'Touché. Wow, Denise. You *are* upset, aren't you? Look, it's the weekend. Forget about the Wiseman-Hopfgartens.'

'I can't. All the unanswered questions in this file are really bothering me.'

'Well, put it down. It's not achieving anything. What else do you want me to do? We can't do anything until the court grant the power to enter and search the Wiseman house for the child.'

'But we need to extend it. Add some details.'

'What are you talking about?'

'I'm reading directly from the guidelines here. *If the applicant believes there may be another child on the premises which is to be searched, who ought also to be the subject of an EPO, an order should be sought authorising a search for that child as well. Where the name of the second child is not known, s/he should be described as clearly as possible in the order.*'

'Denise, my darling, I love you dearly, but you aren't making any sense.'

'Philip, according to this teacher, there are two children in there.'

Now it is Philip's turn to suck against his teeth. 'What?'

'Not one but *two* children, according to the piece of paper in front of me now.'

'No kidding.'

'Double kidding, actually.'

'Not funny.'

'A head teacher that I know of by reputation has been doing her own little bit of private investigation. Two girls. Neither of whom seem to have ever attended any kind of nursery or primary school. The elder child has a name, Avril, and should have started secondary school by now. The younger, whose name isn't mentioned as far as I can see, should have gone into Year 1 last September, by this head teacher's calculations.'

'Crikey Kontiki,' Philip says.

Denise recognises this expression as a peculiar kind of Philipism saved for the most severe moments in life – when other people might be driven to use a harsher expletive. 'I thought that might get your attention. I'm also certain that they *are* resident at the Wiseman address.'

'All right. You're forgiven for being an interrupting cow. But we still can't do anything over the weekend. Let's go along on Monday and find out.'

IV. Hanna

Hanna moves the curtain back, allowing the tiniest crack of light into the dark room. It is enough to confirm her suspicions that the young social worker is back. She adjusts her binoculars and confirms that it is the same number plate as before. Though the car has been parked further away, perhaps in an attempt to approach her unawares and catch her off guard. Hanna smiles. Old Beige Trousers will have to be smarter than that.

But she isn't Beige Trousers today. The social worker has changed her suit: a skirt this time, but still the bland beige corporate uniform with its misguided attempts at femininity through a lens of male construction. Hanna sighs. How foolish some people are. Too foolish to even begin to bother educating.

This time though, she is not alone. She has a colleague with her.

'Male, slightly older than her. But I think I can handle them,' she whispers into the phone, speaking to John, her partner, and for the benefit of the audio recording.

She decides that today will be a 'no response' day. Sometimes she makes a mistake and allows the movement of the curtain to be seen outside. Sometimes she opens the door to allow her voice to be heard, but never so that she can be seen directly. Both techniques usually work to deter unwanted interference. No one else ever enters the house. What right do they have to do that? The footage of Beige Trousers trying to illegally enter her property has already had several hundred views and has been shared a few times – not to mention inspiring some vitriolic comments. She wonders if the star of the show has any idea that she is a mini hate figure online. Perhaps she might back off more if she did.

The letter box rattles and a folded piece of paper is thrust through it. Hanna is tempted to leave it with the other garbage in the hall, but it is always best to know what you're up against, even if you have no intention of succumbing to their foolish requirements.

She notes with some amusement how the language of the communications she receives from social services and various other 'authority' organisations escalates in terms of threat. It would make a good thesis, actually. Most of the organisations have limited powers to do what they say they will anyway, so the family is always safe – and if Hanna knows anything it is the law, especially the law relating to personal rights.

She knows a great deal about how to delay proceedings. She knows how to make a bureaucratic nuisance of herself. She knows how to play one organisation or department off against another until nothing is done. She knows how to galvanise the support of like-minded political progressives that she is in contact with to challenge inequality and unfair intrusion.

But she also suspects now that the real fight has begun. She can hear them outside, talking earnestly on the doorstep, even though there will be no show today.

'I'm sure she's – they – are in there.'

'Me too. Do you think we could see if there is a back entrance? Try and gain access that way?'

'Well, far be it from me to attempt to give my own supervisor advice, but I wouldn't attempt to access her property at all, given what happened to me last time. This woman knows her rights. She'll have you arrested for trespassing and a video of your criminal activity will be on the six o'clock news, complete with running commentary.'

'Fine. Then we let the court do its work.'

'But what happens if they simply don't attend the court hearing?'

'Then *she* will be arrested, as simple as that.'

'And it will be her we see on the six o'clock news.'

Perhaps I underestimated you, Beige Trousers, thinks Hanna. *Perhaps you aren't so foolish after all. Maybe I will give you the benefit of the doubt. Perhaps you are a stronger catalyst than I gave you credit for.* An empty cereal box lies tossed aside on top of a mound of rubbish nearby. She tears a piece from a corner of it and scribbles on the grey cardboard before thrusting it through to the outside world.

It reveals the hyperlink that carries the attempted entry footage.

V. Denise

'At least it's a form of communication. A sign that she's rattled.'

'Philip, you're not helping. And she's not the one who's rattled. I am.' Denise knows that she doesn't come off well, given the commentary that accompanies the shaky footage. 'I didn't do anything wrong. She's made it look as though I pushed against the door. I didn't, not really. It's such an unfair representation of what happened.'

'I know that, you know that. It's not going to make any difference as far as social services are concerned. You've written a statement about what happened. It's fine.'

'Easy for you to say. You're not the one who's going viral.'

'Denise-Denise, I think you're getting ahead of yourself here. A couple of hundred views is hardly "viral". You'll have to do a lot better – or a lot worse – if you're desperate to be an internet sensation, my darling.'

'Can't we get it taken down? Can't we get the police involved? It's got to be some sort of character defamation. Libel or slander or something.'

Denise recognises Philip's sigh as the sound of someone who knows that things are beyond their control.

'Well, let's just take her down in court, shall we? And save these poor kiddies from this horror show of a woman.'

Denise knows that the safety of the children is of greater importance than her own reputation, but the whole thing doesn't sit comfortably. The battle lines are firmly drawn now.

It takes weeks and weeks to reach a destination, even after the wheels have been firmly set in motion.

Once bitten, twice shy, Denise continues to make daily visits to the Wiseman-Hopfgarten property, but never again does she overstep a boundary, and the stench that greets her arrival becomes familiar enough that she does not gag every time she opens the car door. Sometimes Philip attends with her, corroborating her meticulous evidence gathering. The result is always the same, though: she is never able to engage Hanna or get a foot in the door. The curtains remain firmly closed whatever time of day they come, though occasionally there is the tiniest of movements, enough to let Denise know that someone is inside. Because the family have not broken the law, the police have no grounds to get in either. Sometimes Denise just waits outside, on the off chance that Hanna or her partner, or one of the children, opens the door. She is always polite, always within the boundaries of the law. She makes enquiries with neighbours, only to rediscover what she already knows: the family are hardly seen, and the curtains are kept drawn all the time. If it wasn't for the mess of the garden and the smell that emanates from the property, they wouldn't be seen to be causing any problem. They keep themselves to themselves, which makes them something of an enigma in the local area. People are curious about quite what goes on behind closed doors.

As Denise suspected, it is quickly confirmed there are indeed two children. Avril is the elder sister, now aged 14. Sky is her younger sibling, aged nearly six, and their lack of formal education, plus the family's lack of compliance in addressing the requests of social services, means that they are very definitely considered at risk.

Denise treads very carefully indeed. She follows the local authority and government guidelines to the letter, supporting the EPO application with formal documentation giving notice on the parents for not providing adequate information about Avril and her sister's education. But even in an 'emergency', things take time. By the time the case finally gets to court, Denise has logged more than 80 visits to the property.

Denise also liaises with the local housing association who, like social services, are also trying to get into the residence and, like the social services team, keep writing letters that elicit no response. They have grounds to get, and have applied for, a warrant to access the property, but it has not been granted because, as Becky at the housing association reveals, John Wiseman has some sort of disability.

'I'd like to be sympathetic, but my patience has run out. He uses it to make sure that we can't do anything. Any attempt to move forward meets with an accusation of discrimination. I'm telling you, these two are bright and informed and dangerous', Becky says, her conversation taking on a gossipy tone.

But, as Philip predicted, Hanna is indeed forced to attend the court hearing – which takes place on a bitterly cold day. The children are both sent to school on the day, too, for a half day of induction. Neither have clean uniforms or food, but school is the only environment that can offer them safety while John and Hanna attend court. They don't seem to have friends who can help them out, and the children need to be attending school anyway. They are collected by taxi in the morning, and the couple are collected an hour later in disability transport, escorted by two social workers, colleagues of Denise and Philip.

Outside the family courtroom, in freezing temperatures that mean she can see her own breath on the air, Denise gets her first proper glimpse of the woman that she has imagined for months. Hanna Hopfgarten is perhaps in her early thirties, but has the lined face of an older woman, creases worn in by the permanent frown of bitterness she seems to wear. Her features are small and sharp: she has a pointed nose and chin. What might have once been blonde hair is long and dreadlocked, and pulled back into a sort of ponytail, so wild and unruly that it has to be tied with a sheath of fabric rather than a little elastic. In the corridor, and later in the court, her eyes dart about everywhere so that Denise has the sense of a wild animal, caged and desperate.

Her partner, John Wiseman, is a complete contrast. So much so that Denise struggles to see how they could be together. Just what the hell is their story? As Becky at the housing association mentioned, Mr Wiseman does indeed have a mobility disability, and arrives in a wheelchair. He is much older than Hanna, perhaps in his late fifties, but seems just as careworn. Unlike her, he wears a shirt and tie for the hearing, and is therefore at least playing the game of respectability. Denise is surprised to discover that he was once a university lecturer, not just at prestigious universities here, but also in America, and has published a number of important papers. The family courtroom is much less formal than a traditional courtroom, more like a mini lecture theatre or conference room. John Wiseman seems more relaxed than he should. Certainly not fazed in this environment – nothing like the anxious families that Denise more regularly deals with when things reach court level. His assured manner and his smarter appearance give him the kind of credibility in court that Hanna, on the other hand, seems to seek to deliberately subvert. When she walks across the carpet to take her place in the courtroom, Denise notices that she wears military boots and combat trousers – as though she really is entering a battleground.

They have elected to represent themselves, even though plenty of independent support and guidance was on offer. They are both articulate and measured, and neither appear concerned by the fact of having to give evidence to a judge directly. It is a private hearing, so there are only a small number of people in the room, but the judge and the other court staff struggle with the odour that emanates from the couple. It is a diffused version of the stench that Denise has grown used to, but even she struggles with the sickliness of it filling the confined room. The court proceedings take several hours, and even though it is a cold day, no one complains about the open windows.

Eventually an 'S20' is served, a code that everyone connected with social services immediately understands. In essence, it is an order that gives the local authority the power to provide accommodation for the children on the grounds that they do not have somewhere suitable to live.

The S20 is sometimes called 'voluntary care' or 'voluntary accommodation', because generally parents must agree to the child being accommodated. Denise is extremely surprised that permission is willingly granted by Hanna Hopfgarten and John Wiseman. Given all the resistance that they have put up so far, it seems peculiar for them to concede on this – such an enormous step. As they leave the hearing, Hanna turns and fixes her eyes on Denise in a way that forces Denise to flinch and look away, even though she is determined not to. Hanna flares her nostrils, and Denise is once again reminded of an animal, a bull preparing to charge, perhaps. There is a frightening volatility about this woman, and such a look of complete hatred and hostility in those dark, beady eyes that Denise finds herself taking an involuntary step backwards, backing into the row of desks behind her with a clatter. The couple are to be kept in a side room until the children have been collected from school.

Once John and Hanna have exited the room, Denise gives a little involuntary shiver – to shake off the curse that wild look seemed to contain.

Get over yourself. She's just an ordinary woman. She can't do anything to you. Denise finds herself having to coach herself through the business of making her way out of the building and on with the rest of her day.

Philip is waiting for her back at the office. 'Congratulations, Denise-Denise. Your instincts were absolutely spot on. Good job you're such an interrupting cow, frankly.'

'Oi, less of that!' Denise gives her boss a friendly punch on the arm in response. 'Thank you. Though judging by the look Hanna Hopfgarten gave me as she left the courtroom, I have a feeling that this is far from over with her. It's only the first step.'

'But a big one.'

'They were surprisingly acquiescent, given all the barriers that they've put in the way so far. I just can't help feeling that it's some sort of trap. She seemed poised and ready to spring.'

'Not surprising, is it? You're taking her children away. But think about it. By agreeing to the Section 20 they volunteer the handover of the girls, and this gives them certain rights. It gives them power.'

'That's what I'm worried about.'

'Well, don't. You've won the first skirmish, and remember that it's the children that are at the heart of this. You're acting in their best interests, and you have the court on your side. I'll come with you to meet the children from school, and we'll have the police on standby should we need.'

'Environmental Health might be more use, judging by the smell. I feel like I've been gassed.'

'So I hear. The driver wound down all the windows in the car on the way there. Never mind the sub-zero temperature. At one point, you know Collette, who's pregnant, had to stop the car and be sick.'

'I'm not surprised. Seriously, Philip; I've never seen anything like them before. I wonder what the hell we're going to find behind that front door.'

VI. Hanna

Hanna has one hour until her children will be collected from school by the social workers, and it will be a minimum of eight days before she is able to see them again. This gives very little time for additional preparation, but it is the outcome that they all expected, and many of the arrangements have already been made. Avril and Sky have both been well briefed about the nature of the 'holiday' they are about to take, and some of their special possessions have already been stowed in small suitcases in the bedroom. Hanna has supervised the packing.

'If the worst happens, try not to let the social workers enter the property if you can help it,' Hanna advised Avril in the morning, before the hearing. 'You know the tricks.'

Not letting the social workers through the front door isn't the only thing that Avril has been carefully briefed on. The battle has been lost, but it is only one action in the bigger war. This isn't over. In fact, it is only the beginning.

VII. Denise

Denise finds herself in another altercation with a kerb when she pulls up to the school gates, Philip wincing in the passenger seat.

'Tell me you have, in fact, passed a driving test?'

'Very funny. I thought you were here to help.'

'Then help I shall. Would you like me to pull your hubcap away from the concrete by the brute force of my bare hands?'

'Don't kid yourself. There's nothing brutish or forceful about you.'

'If that, Denise-Denise, is a challenge to my manhood, then I feel that I should be reporting you on the grounds of sexual harassment.'

'I'll see you in court, then.'

The senior classes finish ten minutes before their junior counterparts, so they wait in reception for Avril first.

'Why do the older ones have a shorter day? That seems weird,' Philip observes while they're waiting.

'I think they have fewer breaks, so it isn't really a shorter day. And I think it's so big brothers and sisters can pick up younger siblings. It's quite community-minded, if you ask me.'

When the final bell goes, Denise's warmest smile is met with a challenging stare. Avril's jaw line is pointed and immovable, like her mother's.

'So, how was your day?' Denise asks as they stand with Avril in the playground where her sister will shortly be led out by her class teacher a few minutes later.

They are a very awkward few moments.

'No comment.' Avril behaves like a suspect in a television crime drama. She refuses to engage and plays the sullen teenager with aplomb.

Philip raises an eyebrow at Denise and they share a look that seems to say, *what do you expect?*

Avril is tallish for 14, but scrawny-looking, as though she is underfed. She doesn't reek in the same way that her parents and house do, but there is an unpleasant odour surrounding her nevertheless, a further diluted version of the smell that Denise has designated the 'Wiseman Whiff'. Denise is glad that they are in the open air for now, but is acutely conscious of the fact that they will all soon be in her car. She wishes that she had thought to buy an air freshener. Denise notes that Avril has kept the top button of her shirt done right up, but it doesn't hide the fact that she is unwashed. There is a tidemark round her neck. One that signals the kind of caked-in dirt that will no doubt require a great deal of exfoliation to lift.

When Sky emerges, Philip gives a sharp intake of breath and emits a 'Crikey Kontiki', before Denise digs him in the ribs to shut him up and prays that Avril hasn't heard. At least she knows that Philip is as shocked as she is by Sky's appearance.

'Hi, Sky,' Denise says, brightly.

'Remember. You don't have to talk to them,' Avril intervenes. 'They can't make you.'

Sky moves her head slightly, a nod.

'You know why we're here, don't you?'

No response.

'So – did you have a good day at school? What did you do?'

Sky fixes her eyes firmly on her sister, as though Denise isn't speaking at all.

'Well, I hope it wasn't too bad. It's a difficult time, so we're going to make things as easy as we can. Now, my car's the red one—'

Avril gives a snort of derision, as though the car somehow isn't up to scratch. Denise swallows, and after another couple of attempts at small talk, gives up and leads them all to her car. The journey back to the Crickleborough estate takes place in silence.

Denise opens the front door with Avril's key and backs away as agreed.

Avril has five minutes to get some essentials. Philip positions himself at the rear of the house in case Avril tries to run. Denise tries to chat with Sky. 'It's a pretty name, Sky. Much nicer than my name, Denise.'

Avril has pushed the door to behind her, but it remains open just a crack, the farthest Denise has ever seen into the house, despite the 80-odd visits.

What she sees in the hallway shocks her more than anything else she has witnessed in her six-year career in social work, and gives her a tiny glimpse into the strange existence that the girls have survived in their short lives. But it isn't until they have been placed in care that the true horror is revealed.

PART TWO:
Louise

Chapter One

It takes all my patience and powers of persuasion to induce Lily to finally leave the house. I stand in the doorway for a moment or two and watch her walk along the road. I notice how she drags her feet initially and turns to look back over her shoulder a couple of times, but then speeds up as she nears the corner, lifts her head and embraces the day.

Lily is our long-term foster child. She has come so far in the few years she's been here with us. And yet I'm not sure if she'll ever manage to leave for school on time, no matter how early we start the day. We've tried setting the alarm a little earlier and advancing the onset of the morning process and procedures, but it makes no difference. She could have all the time in the world and she'd still be late.

There will be a last-minute dash to the loo, or she's forgotten her water bottle – which I've likely already filled and put in the side pocket of her school bag, but she'll still go hunting for it. She'll suddenly remember some vitally important toy up in her bedroom that absolutely must come with her to school. I think they're all just delaying tactics that probably stem from her attachment to me and Lloyd, my husband – but also to the life that she lives here in our house, a life that is so different from her former existence. Who could blame her for wanting to stay at home and relax? Nevertheless, we know it's important that we instil in her a respect for learning. She must come to appreciate the power of education, as well as the joys and comfort of home. It's important, too, that she immerses herself in the social side of school and finds a way to negotiate her way through the complex business of making and keeping friends of her own. For all the good and bad that they can bring to a young person, her relationships are hers to forge and manage. I feel hopeful these days that we're through the most challenging phases with Lily. We're at the stage now where we can see visible results of our perseverance – as in the way she walked down the road a moment ago. Despite all the trauma and adversity she's experienced in her short life, she's managed to settle down and find an equilibrium of sorts. Of course, we still have the odd bad day, the odd tantrum or refusal, and we have no idea how long that may last. Maybe forever. I hope not.

I breathe out a little sigh: enough contemplation and reflection for one morning. The day's starting gun is about to be fired.

On your marks, get set, go.

I make my morning sprint around the house, grooving a well-worn track: turning off lights, pulling back curtains, opening windows, shaking out duvets and gathering laundry off the floor (or, in Lily's case, socks off her craft table – the mind boggles). We still have much work to do with our long-term foster child, but time has taught me to let things like that go for now, or it will gnaw away at me and I will overreact. In the grand scheme of things, where she discards her clothes isn't that big a deal. It's strange, but no worse than the floor, and only adds a moment to the well-worn routine. I get the washing machine and dishwasher both on, top up food and water in the animal bowls, and take my last slurp of coffee for the first part of the day. I'll have a coffee break mid-morning, but I don't want the coffee shakes and a headache by overdoing the caffeine intake too soon.

First race done, I head to my studio to begin the paid work of the day.

My studio is my solace. It's the single room in the house where I can shut myself away and forget about housework and domestic demands. Its high ceilings are flooded with light from large windows, even on the cloudiest of days. It seems to me to be full of colour and life. There are plants everywhere: ferns and trailing leaves and hanging spider plants birthing their babies. They jostle for space with what some people might call 'clutter', but I prefer to describe as 'inspiration'. Amidst the canvases and jars of brushes and paints are all sorts of objects and curiosities – things that have just found their way here. Plastic containers on the walls house collections of stuff: whatchamacallits and thingamabobs grouped together in a filing system the secrets of which are known only to my brain.

Yesterday evening I sat in bed with my laptop, working until quite late on the tedious business of 'life admin' – in order to carve out today, the whole day, for painting only.

I'm beginning to embark on pastures new in my artistic life. After a recent visit to Tate Modern I have had a calling from the spirits of dead artists to do abstract art. That's how I feel anyway. I've always been a little bit scared of abstract art in the past – at the same time I've always loved it. A naïve part of me used to think it was an easy way out of more complex drawing and painting. It was subject matter that didn't require skills in things like hands and feet – or faces.

I've done portraits of people and animals for years: compositions that require a degree of verisimilitude. And now, something deep within my creative soul seems to want to make abstract art.

If I really stop to analyse it, I think I also believed that it was 'men' who occupied the abstract art space, but not today, because – well, why should they? I have had my calling and now I shall respond.

I begin by opening my sketchbook. I stare at it for a few moments. The blank page is problematic in writing and art. I decide that I need some music to get me going. I put on 'Young, Gifted and Black' by Bob and Marcia. I love this song. It lifts my mood, making me joyful as it has done for years. My teacher at primary school used to play it to us, and it reminds me of my happier moments in Oxford as a child.

I dance in the corner of the studio where there is more space (and where people from outside who sometimes glance in can't see me and my moves), before eventually settling down to do some work. More reggae accompanies my own rhythms. I paint shapes on abstract cut-outs. I have called my most recent work 'Paradoxes' because, after researching and campaigning for children in the care system and reflecting on my own experiences, 'paradox' is a good word for the world.

I drift away into a glorious artistic flow of consciousness. Pretentious, moi?

A ping goes on my laptop. Just like a goldfish, I forget all about my abstract paradoxes and speed-read a referral for siblings looking for foster care. I feel something inside: a fluttering of emotion, excitement, something. I don't know quite why a referral can evoke so much response. I guess it's because human lives are up for grabs. Something hangs in the balance, and we may or may not be part of what happens next.

Foster carers are not all the same. We aren't made from the same mould. We are all very different, have different reasons for what we do, and bring with us our own style of parenting. Mine, I like to think, is pretty easy-going and liberal. Why wouldn't it be? It's in my nature to be that way. But some carers run their households like military operations. It's often more of a need in the carer than the children themselves. It's just a lottery – pot luck for these children as they ping into foster carers' mailboxes. It often comes down to which foster carers have 'empty beds'. Oh, I can't tell you how much I hate that expression, how uncomfortable it makes me, but it's the one used by children's social care, and so we are rather stuck with it. But we aren't running a hospital or hotel – this is our home.

As I look down the referral I can tell instinctively, as that fluttery feeling continues, that I'm just about to say yes.

The referral doesn't actually say a lot. This is not always a good sign. Over the years I have learnt to read what is not there, to see and hear what isn't said. Or to decode what is there in black and white. Adjectives like 'lively', when applied to a child, can often mean 'hard work'. On this referral there is no mention of anything to do with what the children themselves are like. There are no 'character' words at all. I am always intrigued by a mystery. What it does say is that they have hardly been to school or had much life experience. There are two girls, referenced as AW and SW. The elder one is 14 years old. The younger sister is six. Quite a big age gap. My first thought is to wonder whether they have different dads. I keep on reading. According to the referral, they have the same father. He is older than their mother, and not in good health. It's enough to pique my interest. We are lucky enough to have the room to be able to take siblings from time to time – and if it stops them from being separated unnecessarily, then all to the good.

Whoop! I feel excited. It might just bring on another little dance around the studio. I turn the music up once more.

Chapter Two

Action stations! We get the call from Maz, our new supervising social worker.

'As we thought. They have a Section 20, so expect the girls at around 6pm this evening. I'll be at your house just before – we have a lot of paperwork to do.'

It never changes. New arrivals to our home are always exciting.

Our house is ready. I knew two days ago that the girls had a court date and might need a placement straight away. I know very little about them other than that.

Lily is excited. She misses Stella, a recent foster placement of ours, very much – though they do occasionally chat on the phone. They grew very close. We've had other children stay since, but we've had a little break for a few weeks. It wasn't entirely our choice, but we are in a bit of a changeover period. Dave was our previous supervising social worker, but he left the profession to open a floristry business with his wife. We are settling in with his replacement, Maz. We have met her twice now, and received a few emails from her. She seems fine, says all the right things, but it's too soon to tell. As experience has taught us, we cannot judge until we are tested. Foster carers are tested by the children in their care – and sometimes more so by the bureaucracy and processes that are activated by a child's behaviour.

So, we will see – but so far so good. I like the way she has been upfront about the possibility of us being needed at short notice today. Forward planning, and all that.

The boys, Jackson and Vincent, are less excited than Lily, mainly because it is two girls who are arriving. Girls bring nothing relevant to their lives of computer gaming, an existence that is generally accompanied by the sound-track of rap and hip-hop music.

'One's going to be a teenager. She'll mess up our bathroom with mountains of make-up and products,' Vincent complains. He has a dread of teenage girls – we've fostered a few over time.

'And *issues*,' Jackson adds, in a grown-up tone.

I have a sudden, surreal image of our new arrivals filling up our bathroom with 'issues'. I have no way of knowing that they are about to fill much more than the bathroom during their time with us.

I have prepared a selection of meals for the two girls. They will have had a long, emotional day and will either be starving or will not eat at all. But I have covered all options, from chicken nuggets and chips to nibbly snacks, with a spaghetti bolognese thrown in for good measure.

The clock shows that it is nearly half past five already.

The boys have disappeared but Lily, who probably remembers her own arrival straight from court, has prepared a basket of toys that Sky may like to play with.

I am always impressed by Lily's thoughtfulness on days like today. She has an innate kindness that surfaces more and more. We have fewer tantrums from her now. In the beginning there'd often be moments where she would become distressed very suddenly, for no surface reason that was easy to discern. But there is always a reason for these kinds of traumatic outbreaks. There is still much we don't know about Lily's life before, and much that we will never know. It's her story, after all. My role, along with the rest of the family, is to do as much as possible to help Lily, and the other children in our care, to regulate themselves in those volatile moments. If we can manage to teach them that much, then I hope that eventually they will find ways to understand and manage their trauma.

Maz rings the doorbell. I am impressed by her punctuality. She gets another tick from me.

'Lloyd, she's here,' I call out, unnecessarily, to my husband (he's not deaf, but it gives me the illusion of being in control).

Maz brings her warm smile in with her, and pretends to run through the door like an athlete sprinting from the starting blocks. It is both ridiculous and endearing at the same time.

'This is always exciting,' she says, echoing my thoughts from a few moments before.

'It is,' I agree. But my excitement is tempered by an overhanging cloud of concern for the children, and for their family, and for the horrible day they have probably all had. To have been served a Section 20, the parents must have been struggling in a big way. And for the sisters, it is likely to be even more stressful and confusing. They are leaving all they have ever known and are having to deal with the business of coming to a strange home with strange people.

Lloyd welcomes Maz and busies himself pouring her a cup of tea and distributing biscuits. Lily spots the biscuits before barely a rustle from the packet – some sort of super-sense has kicked in. She approaches Lloyd wide-eyed, as if to say, 'Please sir, can I have *one*?' She'd make a good Oliver Twist. There are some archaic words for people like this, due a revival, I think: 'smell-feast' and 'lickdish'. Most children enjoy sweet treats, but none more so than the child who has been deprived of food. In Lily's case, her subconscious mind seems to have decided that she is playing catch-up and needs to make up for the lost biscuits, cakes and ice cream of her past. There is much to discuss about the arrival of Avril and Sky, though Maz explains that information about their background is fairly limited, as the family haven't been very co-operative. They are nice names, though. Avril sounds a little bit French, and Sky puts me in mind of hippies. With little to go on, it is tempting to play guessing games – but it is just that: guessing. Perhaps there is some European heritage, or perhaps the parents are a little bit alternative. We move through the paperwork quickly and I can't help glancing at the clock as the seconds tick by to six o'clock. And then tick by some more.

Whatever is happening with Avril and Sky, they are taking much longer than we thought. Eventually Maz calls the children's social worker to see where they are and what's going on.

Maz reports back that they have left their house after gathering a few essentials and are on their way, but they still have more than an hour of journey time.

Lloyd is restless. We know each other's mannerisms so well that I can tell that he is thinking about all the work that he has to do, and could have been doing in the time we have already been waiting. As a freelance graphic designer, he has the flexibility of working from home – as I do, with my artwork and writing.

I make it easy for him. 'You go. Use the hour. We'll wait here until they arrive. It doesn't need both of us for the time being.'

I can see the relief in his face as he makes his exit.

When you work from home with flexible time, it's easy to work longer and longer hours. When we both began doing it, we thought that working from home would be easier because we wouldn't spend so much time in unnecessary meetings – meetings that come with that sinking feeling of knowing that there is far more talk than action. We are both 'doers' who would rather get on with things than discuss them. At the forefront of tech developments, Lloyd's industry shifted to online conferencing long before a pandemic made us all familiar with Zoom. He has more than mastered the art of the mute button and continuing to work on other things while appearing on his screen. His clients are all lovely. When I walk past his studio, I smile at the sound of coffee cups rattling and familiar voices filling the room. I can't help feeling that he has his work-life balance a bit better than mine.

Eventually, at around eight o'clock, the doorbell rings. I get up slowly. Not only has all the earlier excitement dissipated somewhat, but I am mindful of one social worker in the past who once reported on my 'eagerness to get to the door' as though it was a problematic aspect of my character. I know that a random statement like that can be interpreted in a number of ways, but seeing it written down in black and white like that has remained with me as a reminder that as foster carers, our actions are judged all the time. I try to moderate my behaviour as much as possible and suppress the more flamboyant parts of my personality. Sometimes that feels bland – but it gives less opportunity for things to be written down and judged.

The boys' heads appear at the top of the stairs. Lily is on dog duty, keeping our pair of Jackawawas, Dotty and

Douglas, under a degree of control so as not to overwhelm our visitors. Lloyd comes out of his studio and heads towards the kitchen in preparation. Though the house has plenty of rooms, the kitchen is at the heart of it, and always serves as the 'reception' when anyone arrives at the house.

I get to the door, where two silhouettes are outlined in the night light of the porch – an image that I remember so clearly, even a few years later, because they make a bizarre, contrasting picture. One is tall and thin, the other short and round. I have never seen such a curious pair.

I open the door and welcome the girls.

Behind them are two social workers who look a little tense. First through the door is the tall, thin Avril; I can barely see any of her features, hidden beneath an outsize black hoodie, and the long brown hair that hangs like a curtain across her face. I notice a little bit of skin that manages to look both red and patchy, but also pale. She has a kind of androgynous shape, all angles. In her thin hand is a dark brown suitcase, old and battered and stained. It looks more like a prop from a theatrical production than something a teenager might carry. The way she struggles with the case exacerbates the frailty suggested by her slight figure. I take it from her gently and place it in the hall. She looks at it anxiously. Perhaps it contains a loved teddy or toy.

'We'll take it up to your room in a moment,' I assure her. 'Come on in and get yourself settled first.'

Maz also greets Avril, ushering her into the kitchen to the sound of barking dogs. They are so tiny that their bark seems far bigger than they do. They are more likely to lick you to death than anything else, but I am conscious that it can be overwhelming for unsuspecting newly arrived guests.

Next through the door is Sky. She is clutching a tatty

bundle of fabric that I quickly realise *is* a soft toy. My best guess would be a zebra, but it has clearly seen better days. That is not what captures my attention, though. I have honestly never seen such a round child before in all my days. Not in real life, anyway. I have read articles in magazines about obesity, and seen pictures of outsize children on the news, but Sky is in a different league. Her face is moon-round, and her head sits on her shoulders without any suggestion of neck. She is extremely overweight, so much so that she might actually be wider than she is tall. Her proportions look more like a reflection in a hall of mirrors than a real-life shape. But she is no reflection; she is very real indeed. I have to move the hall stand out of the way to allow her to pass. The name 'Sky' conjures light and airy, insubstantial. If ever a child was misnamed it is this one.

I notice that her hair is a strange mix of grease and dryness, mixed up with knots that look like dreadlocks.

There is something else about these two girls that I was not prepared for: the smell. It almost makes my eyes water as she goes past, and though I try not to let any reaction show, I can't help wincing slightly.

Last come the two social workers, one female, one male: Denise and Philip. Denise offers me a thin-lipped smile and comes in behind Sky. Philip seems to be shivering in a thin coat. 'Brrr,' he says, rubbing his hands together. 'That was a chilly ride.'

'Oh,' I say, looking at the car parked outside. 'Is your heater broken? Come through to the kitchen. It's nice and warm in there.'

I close the door and watch Sky shuffle awkwardly, in a filthy purple coat, towards Maz. Maz's expression is smiling and warm and I don't know how she manages to maintain it.

She does well not to gag as she greets this strange child. I am now gasping for air in the corridor behind them.

We all go into the kitchen. Lily clocks Sky and I see that Sky makes eye contact in return. That's good.

'Perhaps you two could go through to the other room to say hello and get to know each other,' I suggest, knowing how hard it can be for a young child to feel comfortable around strange adults.

Lily is pleased about this, and little Sky screws up her expression into what I think is a smile – her mouth is quite hard to see properly, all scrunched back into her round face.

They head to the sitting room closely followed by two wagging, curious dogs. Not just close; I notice that in fact, both dogs' noses are almost stuck to Sky's legs and coat. Some at least are enjoying the smell, even if they are of the canine variety.

Lloyd makes hot drinks for the two social workers, who look like they are beginning to defrost – but they nod understanding when I find myself throwing open the conservatory door to let some air in. A few seconds of the girls' presence has provoked a great desire for fresh air in spite of the chilly night. I can only imagine that a long car journey must have been horrendous. No wonder they look cold.

'Not a broken heater, then,' I say.

Philip gives me a little wink. Denise gives me the tight-lipped smile again. We understand each other.

Avril sits on a chair at the end of the kitchen table. Her thin body is shrouded in folds of black hoodie and all that is visible of the girl herself is her thin nose, protruding through hair. Her body is hunched up defensively in the chair, and she turns her head away from the circle of adults in the room.

'Would you like a hot chocolate, Avril?' Lloyd asks.

'No,' she says, gruffly.

While Lloyd gets everyone settled around the kitchen table I pop into the sitting room to see what is going on. Lily sits on the floor, close to Sky at the toy basket. Lily turns to me and makes a grimace. I smile back and make what I hope is a reassuring face.

Sky is absorbed in the basket of dolls and teddies. The dogs' noses remain firmly attached to Sky, who still has her coat on and sits cross-legged with Dotty's head jammed into her crotch. This makes me feel somewhat uncomfortable, though doesn't seem to bother Sky.

'Dotty!' I call, but she ignores me – she has something far more interesting to engross her. I feel the need to intervene, so I pick her up. As I get close, the smell hits me like a fist.

I take Douglas too, and bring them both into the kitchen. Now they congregate round Avril's legs.

I put the dogs out in the garden. They do not like this at all, and protest vehemently with loud whines and barks. They will have to be ignored for now. What on earth have we invited into our house?

I join the table of social workers and paperwork. Avril hardly moves her head at all, but it hangs low down. I feel for her and sometimes wonder why we put children through this bit.

'Would you like to go next door with Sky and Lily?' I ask, wanting to release her from her torment.

I catch a look from Maz.

'Perhaps after she has completed this paperwork,' she says, firmly.

Avril shakes her head and then returns to stillness. I wonder if this is a refusal to do the paperwork or to move into the sitting room.

Meanwhile the boys have crept down the stairs and hidden behind the kitchen door.

'Oh, there you are!' I exclaim, as though I haven't seen them position themselves there. I fetch some crisps and drinks. 'Here you are, boys. Take these through to the sitting room and go and say hello to Sky.'

Lily, with her sixth sense of food detection, appears immediately at the kitchen door.

'Yes, there's some here for you and Sky. Come and grab them.'

I sit back down at the table. There is the tiniest of movements from the hooded, bunched figure of Avril in the corner. I think she may have clocked all the food distribution.

'Avril, would you like some crisps? Plenty here,' I say.

Another shake of the head, then a return to complete stillness. It is a very deliberate, tense stillness.

The dogs are yapping to come in from the garden. I know they are cold – and frustrated at not being able to interact with all the visitors. I hope we are going to find a way to wrap this up soon. There can be no sense of relaxing and settling in while we still have three social workers present.

But no, there is yet more paperwork, generated by the complexity of this particular case. On top of the usual documentation, we have to sign forms that confirm that we intend to abide by all the requirements of the Section 20. We are given a standard 'designated authority' form to sign.

'Avril's parents are yet to sign it,' the female social worker, Denise, explains, 'but that's just a formality. You can still operate within its list.'

I give my autograph away in triplicate, then leave the table once more to go and check on the girls. I want to see how they are getting on, but I am also hoping that the gathered adults will take the hint and get on the road for the night. It's nearly ten o'clock, which is almost past my bedtime, let alone the children's.

Lily, as I suspected, is yawning. But Sky still seems wide awake. What a day of new experiences it must have been for her. The social workers have explained that it was also her first day in school. She's had an enormous amount to deal with, but it's not easy to relax when you are away from home for the first time.

'Lily love, why don't you pop up and get yourself ready for bed? Pyjamas and teeth and then you can pop back down for a bit.'

The boys have already disappeared back upstairs. I think they were only down here long enough to inhale their crisps before returning to whatever mischief they are getting up to with all this unexpected freedom and lateness on a school night. They definitely know how to take advantage of a bunch of occupied adults.

I return to the kitchen, delighted to see that Denise and Philip have packed up their bags and have their coats on.

'You've had a long day, too,' I say as I see them to the door. The moment of departure is never a simple exchange of pleasantries, but often offers a crucial piece of information. I know that this is where social workers say what they really need to say and have not been able to in front of a child.

They do exactly this. I am at the door for another quarter of an hour, almost forgetting that poor Maz is still waiting for me in the kitchen. First there are the practicalities.

'We're still sorting additional uniform, but a taxi will be here at 7.15am to take the children to school,' Denise explains. 'Sorry it's so early, but it's quite a long drive.'

I know the firm well and have already decided that these two girls will not be going to school tomorrow; that would be too much after today, after the emotional trauma of leaving their parents and the physical uprooting they have been through. Of course I don't say that, but my mind is already making plans. Foster carers are not officially allowed to cancel these taxis, but I can phone the schools and report their absence, and I can tip the taxi firm off. One of the drivers is a fellow dog walker in the park. I understand that both girls' education has already been impacted by choices their parents have made, but they surely have to feel safe in one environment before they can be plunged into another. We ask so much of traumatised children at times. Plus, it is already so late. At this rate I'm going to end up keeping everyone off school tomorrow if we don't all get to bed soon.

There are more details, though no mention of Sky's weight, which surprises me. I have to allude to the smell though.

'Ah, yes. The Wiseman Whiff,' Philip says, before apologising after a warning look from Denise.

Then we get to the message that the social workers evidently did want to communicate.

'There is likely to be a little friction. Given what we know of the parents, mum and dad will fight to get the children back.' Denise seems to be on the verge of saying something else, but hesitates.

'Particularly mum,' her colleague adds.

'It shouldn't affect you too much of course, but always best to be in the know.' They exchange a look which I am too tired to interpret, and I am just left with an overwhelming feeling of sadness. What a situation to be in. I can't imagine how I would feel if my children were put into care. People will say in a case such as this, particularly where the court has decided to intervene so dramatically, that parents 'deserve' to lose their children. It's never quite as simple as that, in my experience. There is always a backstory: a set of circumstances and then a particular catalyst that spirals a family into tragedy. I always wonder what society could have done sooner to help.

'Thanks for the heads-up. I'll call the lead social worker in the morning to let them know how the girls get on overnight.'

When I get back to the kitchen, I am pleased to find that Lloyd has already sent the boys to bed, along with a slightly more reluctant Lily.

Maz is standing up with her coat on, chatting to Lloyd. She too looks tired.

'Thank you,' I say. 'For staying on with us.'

I don't imagine she gets paid any kind of overtime allowance. I read a survey recently that said the average social worker was doing up to ten hours of unpaid overtime every single week. I can well believe it.

She gives me a tired smile. 'I'll call you in the morning to see how things are.'

Lloyd follows her out to the hallway to see her to the door, which leaves me alone in the kitchen with Avril.

'Long day,' I say. 'You must be hungry. Or thirsty at least.'

She shakes her hoodied head and I have the strangest sensation of speaking to the Grim Reaper. I shake off that fanciful nonsense immediately and run through a few food options that I can rustle up quickly.

Another head shake.

'OK, well, let me know. Would you like to have a look

round the house? I can show you where your room is, and the loo, and where to find everything you might need.'

She gets up from her seat without a word but follows me. We go into the sitting room, where Sky is still wide-eyed and playing on the floor, still with her coat on, I notice.

'We're just having a little tour,' I say. 'Would you like to come and see your rooms?'

Sky is thrilled with hers. She stands in the middle of it and does a clumsy twirl, repeating the words, 'I can sleep here? I can sleep here.' First as if it is a question, then an answering statement. She says it over and over again.

'Yes, you can sleep here,' I laugh. 'Will that be all right? Right. Let's go back down to the kitchen and see about getting the two of you a little drink or something before bed.'

As we are going down the stairs, I hear the sound of my phone ringing. That's odd, I think, for someone to be ringing so late. I wonder if something is wrong.

My phone is lying on the kitchen table. When I reach it I don't recognise the number, but imagine it to be a mistake so late into the evening. By now it is past 11 o'clock.

'Hello?' I answer tentatively.

'This is Hanna. Avril and Sky's mother.'

'Oh, hello,' I say, more than a little taken aback.

'Avril said she would like a jam sandwich.'

'Er, right, jam sandwich; no problem. Yes, I can do that,' I say, caught completely off guard.

She hangs up.

I look at the receiver, then towards Avril, who has rediscovered her earlier position and is sitting in the corner with her hoodie up and her head cast downwards, hands in her lap.

It feels like the oddest moment.

'Jam sandwich, then,' I say, busying myself collecting things from the fridge. I make a sandwich for each of them.

'I'm going to bed,' Avril announces.

I collect her suitcase from the hall and take it upstairs, placing it on the floor in her room. I have already put a fresh towel on the chair.

'Do you need anything else?' I ask.

She says nothing, but opens the case up. Inside are two more soft toys: dirty teddy bears which, like Sky's zebra, have seen better days. There is also an Xbox and some games.

'Have you got a TV monitor?' Avril asks, without looking at me.

'Yes, absolutely. I'll get that for you in the morning.'

'Could I have it now, please?' she says. Her tone is perfectly polite, but I think we both know that she is being rude.

On my way to Sky's room, I call to Lloyd to get the monitor for Avril.

He comes to the foot of the stairs and gives me a querying eyebrow, but obliges. While she is in the bathroom he sets it up.

Back in Sky's room she is twirling round again, still with her dirty purple coat on. What should be a joyful sight is marred somewhat by the fact of her disturbing shape and size. To be so little, so young, and yet this big is incongruous somehow.

'Sky, would you like to borrow some pyjamas?'

She looks at me with a strange expression on her face, mouth twisted as if she has not quite understood.

I hold out a large pair of elastic-waisted leggings and a big, loose T-shirt. 'How about these?' She shakes her head and looks away, before climbing up to lie on top of her bed.

'No problem, whatever you feel comfortable in. Shall I just take your coat to hang it up?'

Another shake of the head. 'No. I sleep in my coat.'

Not here you don't, I think. I am already mentally washing the places in the house that the filthy fabric has been in contact with.

I spend the next half an hour attempting to persuade Sky to give me her coat and clothes so she can put some nightclothes on. I stand outside the room while I think she is getting changed. When I go back, she is still clad in purple. I explain gently why it is a good idea to change for bed. I cajole. I offer to help, in case it is the buttons she struggles with. I cajole, I coax. Finally, I lose patience and resort to bribery, offering her a biscuit. That does it.

I want those clothes off her and in the washing machine. She hands me her clothes in exchange for a cookie, and I can't decide if this is a victory or not. As I fill the washing machine tub, I notice that there are no knickers in the pile, but opt to approach this tomorrow – after a trip to the large supermarket to buy some supplies.

Back upstairs, I ask Sky if she would like to clean her teeth.

She just stares at me as if I have asked her the question in another language.

'We'll work on that tomorrow,' I concede. 'It's very late, so it's time for sleep. Would you like the light on?'

A nod. I place the zebra and her other teddies – that also reek of that ground-in stink of years of accumulated filth – next to her on the bed. Tonight is not the night to try to take them away for washing. She lies down again.

'Good night,' she says, obedient and automaton-like.

'Good night, Sky. I'll check up on you in a few minutes,' I promise. I have a little foreboding, and suspect that tonight is not going to be easy – for any of us. I cannot fathom these two girls; they are as strange as I have ever seen. So far, everything about them screams out to me that I'm going to be in for a ride. I hope it's not too bumpy.

I return to the kitchen to hear the dogs, still yapping away outside. I'm not doing very well tonight; they have been completely ignored in the busyness of the evening's events. They run in enthusiastically – my abandonment of them is forgiven in a moment as they sniff the floor round where Avril was seated in the kitchen, before bounding into the sitting room to do more important investigations at the spot where Sky was positioned. There are exciting new smells to be examined, accompanied by much tail wagging. I leave them to it and decide that it is time to check on Avril.

She is sitting on her bed with headphones on, gaming. She doesn't look up as I stand in the doorway.

'Um, Avril? Could I talk to you just for a moment?'

She removes her headphones with that teenage technique of suggesting that the tiniest actions require the most tremendous effort.

'It's really time to get some sleep,' I say.

She nods. 'Thank you.' But makes no effort to shut down the game.

I can't see exactly what it is she's playing; it might be Minecraft. The children have told me about the 'Survival' mode in the game where the goal is to use the resources of the world to build shelter, find food, and craft tools to help them construct the universe they want to live in. Perhaps that's what she's trying to do: construct at least a virtual universe that she wants to inhabit. I don't really know what to do, and hesitate half in and half out of the room. I will always try to respect the privacy and personal space of any of the children we foster, but somehow she has already claimed this room for herself and I am the one who feels awkward in my own home.

'Um, right then.' I decide that now is not the time to intervene. She must be in a bit of shock after the day she's had. We'll think about establishing some ground rules about gaming tomorrow.

I walk back past Sky's room and open the door a fraction to check on her as I promised I would. She is no longer on the bed, but lying on the floor – and seems to be fast asleep. I don't want to disturb her, and there is certainly no way I can lift her. I get the pillow to put it under her head and cover her with the duvet.

I need some sort of debrief, and I'm glad to see that Lloyd is still up and pottering about, putting papers into piles on the kitchen table.

'The oddest thing happened.' I tell him about Hanna phoning me on my mobile to ask me to make a jam sandwich for Avril while Avril herself was a couple of feet away and had refused everything I offered. 'I mean, I'm not even sure how she would have my number.'

'Well, I guess the Section 20 business means that the parents have to be told where their children are. Maybe the social workers gave her your number.'

'Yes, maybe,' I say, though I can't help feeling that would have been mentioned – especially when they were warning me about how Hanna would fight for the return of her children.

I feel a terrible sense of unease as I try to fall asleep, and even though I am very tired, I toss and turn and can't get comfortable. There is something about that phone call that has unsettled me.

Chapter Three

I am awake early, not entirely sure that I have slept at all. If I did, it was with one eye open, expecting one of the girls to move about in the night. I get up and make some coffee. I take the drinks upstairs and wake Lloyd, who is yawning and frowns when he comes to.

'What's that smell?'

He remembers that we have two unusual children in our care and nods his realisation. There is a whiff of the girls that has permeated the house now.

'I'll open a window.'

'It's January,' he complains.

'Cold or asphyxiation. Your choice.'

'I'll take the cold,' he agrees.

I remember that I left the washing machine running when I went to bed last night, full of Sky's clothes. When I get them out the smell is still strong. Uuggh. Not a success. I put them back in the washing machine and do it again, adding extra fabric conditioner.

Next, I let the dogs out from their crate. Their noses are over everything, sniffing away again, tails wagging gleefully.

My phone is still lying where I left it on the kitchen table last night. I go to put it on charge and notice that there is a text message.

Avril doesn't like her curtains. They give her the creeps. Please sort.

I feel annoyed. Who does she think she is? We're a home, not a bloody hotel.

But I bite my lip and text back, *Thank you for letting me know.* It's a much politer answer than the one that was really in my head, but I don't want to engage. Bloody cheek. Avril must have sent a picture of her room to her mum. This thought also makes me feel uncomfortable.

Another text pings in a few seconds later.

Sky hates the dolls in her room. Dolls give her nightmares. Can you remove them?

It's a perfectly reasonable request, and I know that some children don't like dolls, so I don't know why this annoys me so much. Still, I reply again, *Thank you for letting me know.*

I hate feeling so discombobulated, especially first thing in the morning. My day hasn't even begun properly yet. Grrr. Don't let her get to you, I tell myself. I convert the number to my contacts so I can see when she is calling me. I have already decided that that way I can ignore it.

I go back upstairs and gently open the door of Sky's room. She is still on the floor; her large, round body is half out of the duvet, so I place another blanket over her to keep her warm. She is snoring quite heavily. I would never have believed it was the snore of a six-year-old if I hadn't just seen her doing it with my own eyes. I pull the door to and go in to have a look at Avril. She is sitting up in exactly the same position as I last saw her – with her headphones on, gaming.

She looks at me and gives me a half smile. It is patronising somehow, and also seems to contain a challenge. I don't *like* her, I realise. I never usually think this about a child. Adults, yes. I've got a few on my list that I might say that about, but I've never felt this way about a child before – especially not one I've really only just met. I don't think I could put into words exactly what she makes me feel. There is something menacing about her; something about her presence that makes me feel uncomfortable. I try to brush it aside.

'Morning, Avril,' I say cheerily, determined not to let her see how she makes me feel. She is probably a perfectly nice young woman. Life has dealt her a bad hand. I can make allowances. She needs me to give her a chance. 'Did you sleep okay?'

She nods.

'That's good. I'm glad to hear it. Would you like some breakfast?'

She shakes her head and carries on gaming, conversation over. I have been dismissed. Frustrated, I close the door. I'm not usually outwitted by a teenager. Certainly not by an only-just teenager – I must be losing my touch. But she is certainly pressing my buttons. And she has done nothing that I could even quite put my finger on that could be construed as really objectionable.

I move on to the other children. Jackson is fast asleep. I call his name. 'Time to wake up and get in the shower,' I tell him.

I get a 'yeeeeah' from him, so move along the hall to Lily.

She is rubbish if she has a late night. She is not a morning person anyway, but it is all exacerbated if she doesn't have enough sleep.

'Lily-Lils,' I call. 'Time to wake up.'

She makes a sound of coming to, sort of. But I know her well. If she goes back to sleep and is then running late, she will blame me. 'Lily, have you heard me?' I check. No answer. 'Li-ly? Time to get up.'

'Yes, all right,' she says, groggily. But we have communicated – that's good.

61

Last but not least, I walk up the stairs to the attic room to rouse Vincent. He is always the most cheerful child in the morning.

'Vincent, time to get up,' I call gently.

'Okay, Mum,' and then, 'Morning!'

Well, one out of five isn't bad.

It's still early but I know the taxi will have someone on call, so I give them a ring. The taxi firm know as well as I do that according to the terms of the account with social services, I'm not allowed to cancel a taxi, but we also both know that the social worker may forget or not get time to cancel – so it wastes time and money. This way I can tip them off and not open the door to a cross driver who has wasted his or her ride. Everyone's happy. I have to do an internet search for the number for the girls' school, and leave messages there too.

Over cornflakes in the kitchen, Jackson, Vincent and Lily want to know more about Sky and Avril. I don't blame them – they're a pair that invite curiosity – but I put them off.

'There's plenty of time. They'll be here when you get back this afternoon.'

Jackson sniffs the air. I make no comment. I don't want the children to tell other children that they smell. And if I don't acknowledge it, then it might go away. I know this not to be true, even as I think it. The children are 'morning-processed' quickly and out of the door ready for school, giving me time to rush through the house doing the usual catalogue of chores.

I go to take my phone off charge and notice that Hanna has sent another text.

Avril would like a sandwich.

Oh, would she indeed. I do my best to ignore it. But Lloyd comes into the kitchen after his shower and I show him the text.

He makes a face. 'You need to tell the social workers straight away. We can't have this.'

'Yeah, you're right. I'll wait until I know the social workers are at work, which isn't for a little while yet.'

Meanwhile I go up to Avril's room.

'Avril, would you like a sandwich?' I ask.

She nods.

'No problem. It will be in the kitchen.'

She doesn't come down.

The text message alert goes.

Lloyd, sipping his second coffee, picks up my phone and whistles before reading it aloud.

Avril would like her sandwich in her room.

Now Lloyd is annoyed.

It's so interesting how we feel about any kind of violation to our homes. They are a safe place that cannot be compromised in any way. We both quickly arrive at the same thought and talk over one another.

'This has to stop today—'

'Hanna has to stop this interference.'

By half past nine I gauge that the social workers will have been in their offices with enough time to get their feet under the desk, make some coffee and be dealing with the day's workload. Hopefully not in meetings yet. First, I call Maz.

'... so Avril slept in her clothes while gaming, and Sky slept on the floor after I spent some time persuading her to take her clothes off and put pyjamas on.'

'Things will get easier as they get to know the routines of your household.'

'That's not the tricky bit.' I explain to Maz about Hanna texting. 'I can't really cope with that. It feels like interference, but also more than that. Calculated to wind me up.'

She agrees. 'But as we both know, on a Section 20 the parent has a right to know where their child is. Maybe the children's social workers gave her your number?'

'I don't mind them knowing where she is, but I'm not operating room service here. And shouldn't they have asked? We chatted for ages at the end of the evening. And they seemed nice. Wouldn't they have said that they had done that?'

Next I call the girls' lead social worker, which turns out to be Denise, not Philip. I let her know how they slept, and that I decided they couldn't make it to school.

'The care plan was for them to go to school today—' she starts to say.

'I know that, but there was no way I was sending those two to school today.'

'No, don't worry. I understand. And it's probably best.'

Sometimes it feels like common sense is the unofficial last resort.

I ask Denise about my phone number being given to Hanna.

'Absolutely not, no. We definitely haven't given it to her. We had to tell the parents where Avril and Sky were, but until your call came through this morning I didn't even know your number to give her. Otherwise I would have phoned to explain that we were going to be late.'

She hesitates. 'There were a few delaying tactics when we went to pick up their belongings. It all took much longer than we expected it to.'

'Is there a way that you can ask Hanna not to call me?'

'I'm not sure. While we wouldn't have given it out, now that she has your number, she is entitled to call you to see how the children are. I'm sorry.'

'But Avril has a phone herself and is clearly in regular contact with her mum – so there is no need for Hanna to talk to me directly. We've never been in this kind of situation before.'

Denise is sympathetic, but not very helpful in practical terms. 'I'll talk to my manager, but I don't think there's much we can do. It's the law.' She apologises once more.

I believe that they didn't give out my number. So how the hell did Avril get hold of it?

'The other thing is, we are now handing the case over to a different social work team – the Looked After Children team. As they are no longer Children At Risk. So a new social worker will be in touch soon. I'm sorry.'

'That's the third time you've apologised.'

'Because I'm genuinely sorry. This is one of the oddest cases I've worked on. It took a long time to proceed to this stage. I'd like to be there for them.'

I've written so much about staff turnover and changes in personnel and the lack of continuity at social services that I forget how it must feel on the other side.

'Any problems there is the Out of—'

'Out of hours service. Yes, I know.'

'Anyway,' she says. 'You shouldn't really use it after this week, but you've got my number.'

And Hanna's got mine, I think, as we hang up. And how she got hold of it remains a mystery. It occurs to me that Avril was left alone in the kitchen last night while my phone was on the table. I don't like the directions my thoughts are going in, but I can't help wondering if Avril picked it up last night and worked out the number. Is it even recorded anywhere on the phone? And how would she have got round the password lock?

The phone rings. It's Hanna's number. I hesitate for a moment and let it ring a few times before snatching it back up to answer.

'Hi, Louise. It's Hanna here. I thought I would just say hello properly.'

'Hello.'

'You and I will be friends, I'm sure. I mean, I am not going to give you, the woman looking after my children, a hard time, am I?'

I know in that moment that she *is* going to do just that.

'Can I just ask how you got my number?'

'The social worker gave it to me.'

I know this is not true. She is lying.

'Well, it's lovely to meet you. To talk to you,' I say, even though it isn't. 'And I will look after your daughters well.' She doesn't say anything, and so as a way of reassuring myself I add, 'Until we're advised otherwise.'

It's petty, but to me it makes the arrangement feel temporary. This will just be a brief stay. Because for now, I am not enjoying it one little bit.

Chapter Four

The washing machine has finished, so I take out Sky's clothes. They still smell, so back in they go for wash number three.

I go up to see Sky, who is still asleep and snoring. It really is unusual for a child her age to snore. It must be related to her size, I think. Her poor body is all squashed up on the inside.

Just as I turn to leave the room to let her sleep on some more, she wakes.

Her eyes are sunk into her face, and her mouth is a tiny round button pushed into her enormous cheeks. She turns her head to the side and looks around the room. She smiles and says something that sounds like, 'No flies.'

'No flies on you this morning,' I say, though I have no idea what she means. 'Now, are you hungry? Would you like some breakfast?'

She heaves herself up from the floor.

'Did you sleep on the floor at home?'

'Yes, because the bath was full up.'

Again, I don't really understand what she means. 'Did you sometimes sleep in the bath?' I ask, trying not to frown.

She nods.

Wow, these two are going to be interesting.

She follows me to the stairs, but struggles to hold on when placing her foot on the stair. She seems nervous and tentative, and I wonder if her weight is affecting her balance.

'Do you have stairs at home? How do you manage them?'

'I don't come down them.'

I wonder if she lives in a bungalow and try to hold her arm to help.

She does not appear comfortable with this and pulls away.

'Can I go down in front of you?' I ask. I want to be able to catch her if she falls. She reaches the bottom of the stairs and seems much more at ease, though she walks with her legs wide and turned outwards. It's a sad scene.

I know from experience that when a child first arrives, offering a brand-new diet can cause anxiety and trouble, but I want to know what she's been eating and tackle her weight.

I am acutely aware of the smell still lingering. I remember the peculiar fact of no knickers in the wash and wonder if she has kept them on to sleep in; hygiene in that area certainly needs attention. It does elsewhere too. Her hair is thick with dirt and now that we are standing in daylight, I can see the jumping head lice. The myth that they don't like dirty hair, only clean, is just that – a myth.

There are sores below her chin that merge into her non-neck area, a place where the grime lives and the sweat lingers. Her eyes look tiny – lost in this oversized balloon of a face. She is the most unusual sight, and I am desperate to help, but there are some major issues here and it certainly isn't going to happen overnight.

'What would you like for breakfast?'

'Biscuits.'

I show her the cereal selection instead. She chooses the chocolate ones – an own-brand version of coco-cushions. I'm not sure they're going to help our situation, and they probably contain as much sugar as biscuits, but never mind.

I pull out a chair for her and she sits down with some effort – but she is still smiling. In fact, she has not stopped smiling since she walked in last night. She is a curious thing. They both are. I eye Avril's sandwich, still sitting on the table, untouched. I get a bowl and pour some cereal into the bowl, adding the milk for Sky.

She watches carefully as I make these actions, still smiling. I hand her a spoon.

'Thank you,' she says as she takes it.

Some good work has been done. I can see that. She has had only one day of school – the place where many of the children we look after learn much about politeness and manners. From reading her paperwork, I get the sense that they have been very isolated. I don't think there was any influence from grandparents – who can be another good source of manners. It seems that she and Avril have only been with their parents.

I suspect that there is much more of a story behind these girls. When I spoke to Hanna on the phone, I did detect the trace of an accent, but the conversation was so short I couldn't pin it down. She sounded well educated, though.

I put some cling film over the sandwich and watch Sky tuck into her cereal. She seems delighted by it.

'Have you had this cereal before?'

'No. I saw it on television.'

After the cereal she is evidently still hungry, looking around the kitchen for more. I don't want to deprive her and start a diet on day one with everything else going on. I offer some toast and honey.

She loves this, too.

'Have you had honey before?'

'No. It's nice.'

She really is very sweet and easily pleased. I go to the fridge and lift out two cartons of juice.

'Apple or orange?'

She peers at both cartons and beams. 'Apple.'

I pour a long glass of juice. That too is happily devoured.

'Have you had apple juice before?'

'No. It's lovely.'

She seems strangely happy. Often when children first arrive, they are sad or quiet. Sometimes angry. Sky just seems happy with everything.

'If you've had enough to eat now, would you like to have a bath and wash your hair?'

'No thank you,' she says.

'I won't come in. I'll just run it and leave you to it.'

'No,' she says again, but she is still smiling.

I need to find a way to persuade her. The diet may not be starting today, but we are going to get somewhere with the smell.

'I have these amazing bath bombs that sparkle and smell amazing. They're great fun. If you like you can put one in the bath.'

She beams and nods.

'Okay, I'll show you. Let's go and do this.'

I start the bath running and leave Sky gazing up at the pictures on the bathroom walls while I make a quick detour to our bedroom. We have a trunk where I keep a selection of pants and socks and pyjamas and basics. I dig around to find a packet of girls' pants aged 13 to 14 years. I don't think they will be big enough, but there's more chance than with the five- to six-year-old size. I pull out a pair of leggings, plus socks and a red hoodie that I think will fit. It's difficult to tell.

The bath is filling up nicely. I place the clothes on the floor with a clean towel. In my dressing room drawer I keep ridiculously expensive bath products for occasions just like this. I have never used one – too much glitter for me – but I have never met a girl or young boy who hasn't wanted one in their bath. I bring out a huge peach-coloured bomb full of oils and glitter. It smells good. I suspect that after her reluctance to have a bath, I won't be able to wash her hair today, but if at least she wets it that would be a start.

I make a big fuss of Sky: lots of praise, lots of encouragement. I talk her through the bath bomb and washing and how, when she gets out, to be careful and use the towel and dry properly before she gets dressed.

She beams and nods and I get another quiet, polite 'thank you.'

'Are you sure you wouldn't like me to help?'

By answer, she closes the door behind me, shutting me out.

I stand outside for a moment, waiting to hear the sound of water as she gets in. When it doesn't happen, I imagine that she is struggling to get her clothes off.

'Are you okay, Sky? Is everything all right?' I call.

A quiet 'yes,' but still no sound of water being displaced.

I can still hear the gentle fizz of the bath bomb. Perhaps she is waiting for that to finish. I wait a little longer.

'Are you okay, Sky? Are you in the bath?'

Another quiet 'yes.'

Maybe she just got in very quietly. I head to her room to tidy up, first opening the window to give it a good airing. I leave her for a few more minutes, then pop back, knock on the door and ask if she is okay for a third time.

She opens the door and comes out immediately in the clean clothes, though her hair is dry. One step at a time.

'You look lovely in red,' I say.

She beams and heads back to her room.

I go in and pick up a dry towel and the clean knickers.

The bath bomb looks lovely in the still-clean water. I close my eyes to shut out the disappointment I feel, but it is still early days and I will try again. I look for the dirty knickers, that I am now convinced are a source of the pervasive smell, but I can't see them. I go into her room and gently ask where her knickers are, to which she simply shrugs. Maybe she hasn't got any on.

Chapter Five

Next it's time to tackle Avril. I know that I need to get both girls some new clothes. In the suitcase that Avril arrived with there was an Xbox, headphones, a few games, two teddies (that I'm desperate to put through the washing machine) and nothing much else, as far as I could see. I need to find a way to get her unglued from her room.

I tap on the door. 'Avril, it's Louise. Can I come in?'

There is no answer.

I knock again and enter. She is still on the bed with her headphones on, but this time holding the iPhone rather than the games console. I can just about see her nose under her scraggly hair and hoodie, but enough of her chin to notice that there is a red rash across it. I'm not sure it was there last night, but I didn't get a good enough look to be sure.

'Your sandwich is still downstairs. Would you like to come down and get it? Or have something else for breakfast? Sky's had some cereal.'

'No thank you.'

'Well, it's there if you want it. Then I thought you might like to come shopping.'

'No.'

Just me and Sky, then.

Once Sky is ready, we head off to the big supermarket to find some new clothes. The allowance for the girls won't come through for another week. Experience has shown me that foster carers can lose money pretty quickly by upfront spending. You have to submit receipts – which can go unsupported by the children's social worker's manager, so it's always something of a risk. But we can't wait and wait with nothing. I have learned to start with a cheaper set of clothes until I have the money and I know what the child likes to wear.

We head off up the motorway. There are nearer supermarkets, but I want the 'extra' store that has a large clothing section. As we walk into the building and up the travelator, Sky looks around timidly. She seems a little in awe of the setting.

She gazes up at the lights and lingers at all the areas of merchandise before announcing, 'This is the best day ever.'

My other children will roll their eyes at the thought of going to a supermarket – unless there is a meal deal or small toy included as part of the outing.

'Have you been to a supermarket like this before?'

'No. But I've seen shopping centres on television.'

I'm surprised, but quickly building a picture that this child really hasn't been anywhere very much. I notice that people stare at Sky, or do a double take. She is quite a sight, being so short in such a round little body, and the bright red hoodie makes her stand out even more. I hate myself for it, but have a sharp pang of shame that people might think that she is mine – and that I did this to her. Sometimes as a foster carer, you want to hold up a sign saying 'I am a foster carer' just so that everyone knows. The thought is fleeting: I quickly bring myself back in line, reminding myself that this isn't about me but the child in my care. I hold my head up a little higher and switch instead to feeling immensely protective of little Sky.

We look around at the rails of girls' clothes. I hold a few things up against her half-heartedly, but find nothing that looks like it will actually fit. I look in the adult sizes and find some elasticated leggings that might do if I can turn them up at the bottom. Sky doesn't seem to understand the concept of a skirt, which is a shame. Given her strange shape, a skirt would be far easier to work with. There is no luck with jeans; nothing that looks stretchy enough, and until I solve the knickers dilemma we're not going to be doing any trying on of anything. (The piles of clean knickers continue to go down from Sky's drawers, so I'm now convinced that she is wearing them, yet no dirty knickers appear in the dirty washing. It is most peculiar.) I find a few T-shirts and hoodies in size 13 to 14, but they will come down to her knees. This is going to be more difficult than I imagined when I sailed cheerfully out of the house this morning. It will take some thinking about. Do they even have specialist shops for children of this shape?

For Avril, in her absence, I pick up another black hoodie and jeans, a carbon copy of what she already wears – and some more clean underwear in her size. To my utter surprise, while I am loading up with socks and pants for the others, Sky holds up a coat that is nothing like her original. It has a contrasting lining and a nice shape to the bottom of it. A fashion item, in fact. This gives me hope: she must have been observing other girls. I happily pop it in the basket. Whether I get the money back for this or not, it will be money well spent.

As we go back down the travelator towards the checkout, we get a good view of the rest of the store and its enormous food hall area. Sky stops for a moment in her shuffling tracks to take it all in.

'Wow,' she says.

I nod. It does look vast.

'Is this real?'

I am not sure what to do. Do I walk her round or do I take her back home?

'Can we have a look around?'

My mind is made up for me.

We start walking through the vegetable area. It is a large supermarket, bigger than usual, but I am curious to see what food Sky recognises. Not a great deal, as it turns out. She is amazed by everything, stops to look at colours and different shapes, picks some things up and asks what they are called. She doesn't know what a carrot is, or a lettuce or a cucumber. She does identify a potato.

'Yes, that's a potato. Do you eat those at home?'

'No, but I've had one before. When Mum and Dad were at the hospital a lady called Sylvia looked after me and gave me a baked potato with some cheese on it.'

'We can buy some potatoes and make baked potatoes tonight for supper if you like?'

'I'd like that,' she says. 'It was the best meal I ever had until today.'

'Yes, you had a nice breakfast, didn't you?'

'I like breakfast. We don't have breakfast at home. We just eat any time.'

'Oh. Well, we usually have breakfast, lunch and dinner.' I tell her the times of the meals.

'Can we have some lunch?'

It's a bit early, but if she really is used to just eating when she chooses, then she might well be hungry again already.

We go over to the sandwich section, and I explain that she can choose a meal deal for herself, and another for her sister.

It takes quite a while for her to understand the three-item limit, but eventually she chooses the big triple decker 'all-day breakfast' sandwich for both of them, plus crisps and a bottle of Coke each. I replace the Cokes with Diet Cokes, put the items in the trolley along with our clothes, and continue walking along to the cold fridge area for me.

From what I'm already thinking of privately as the 'Sky shuffle', she breaks into something closer to a run – or at least there is a dramatic pace increase, as she reaches the cold shelves behind me. She touches bags of fresh pasta with something approaching wonderment, picks up sauces, moves on to the pizzas. I am reminded of what it felt like the first time I took our young children to a wildlife park, but that was a special event. This is a day-to-day chore, and I am increasingly struck by how small Sky's world has been up until now, but also how big she is. We continue to walk round. For both of us it is a fact-finding mission. For Sky to find out quite what is out there, and for me – well, I am hoping to get a sense of what she has been used to eating at home. She discovers the crisps aisle, close to the fizzy drinks. She finds the biscuits and cakes. If it is full of sugar or salt, she seems to home in on it.

'Which ones are your favourite?' I ask.

She points at Monster Munch and Quavers. 'I've never seen them in big bags like this before. Is that one big packet?' She is talking about the multipacks of 12 and 24 bags. I am getting a picture that perhaps Sky's food has mostly come from a local small shop or even a newsagents. She is at home in the sweets and chocolate section, and spots Pot Noodles among the rice and dry pasta on the shelves. She's giving me as much to think about as I am giving her this morning.

When we get home, I am hit by the wall of their smell again. It has been diffused to some extent while we've been outside and Sky has been wearing fresh clothes. I put Sky's meal deal on to a plate. I go upstairs with Avril's new clothes and knock on her door. I don't wait for an answer this time but walk straight in – to see that she is still lying on the bed with headphones and phone.

'Hi Avril, we're back,' I say, brightly. I tell her that Sky chose a meal deal. 'It's waiting for you downstairs.' I want to add, 'along with the other sandwich you and your mother demanded,' but I don't.

She looks at me – or at least points the end of her nose that peeps through the curtain of hair in my direction.

'Can I have it in here, please?' she says, ever so politely.

'No.' I have thought about this and am determined to be firm. 'We don't have food in the bedrooms. It's not what we do in this house. It makes the rooms smell.' I am slightly struck by the absurdity of saying this given that we are swamped by the smell they have brought into the house with them.

'Come downstairs,' I say, more gently. 'Just for a few minutes while you eat your food. Then you can come back up here.'

She shifts from the bed, reluctantly.

'Here,' I say. 'I got you these,' and show her the new clothes. She says nothing, but I think she is pleased. The clothes she's wearing are pretty old and grubby, and these are as close as I could find to her 'look.' She follows me down to the kitchen, and tucks into her all-day breakfast sandwich. She is clearly hungry, and eats her food quickly. She knew the first sandwich was down here for her. Was it just a perverse sense of not giving in that has prevented her from coming down for it?

While they are eating, I try to make a few suggestions.

'If you wanted to have a shower, Avril, that would be fine. Probably a good time to do it, before the others come back from school.' I explain the hot and cold buttons and the idiosyncratic settings of the shower in her bathroom.

She finishes her food, mutters 'thank you', and heads upstairs. She hasn't exchanged a word with her sister.

Soon I hear the shower going and I'm pleased. I'm sure that Avril will feel much better after it and it will be nice to get into some clean clothes.

After Sky has finished her food she goes to the loo. I leave her to it, thinking nothing of it until I walk past the door a little while after. A torn piece of toilet roll lies beside the toilet bowl. Not only does she not know quite how to use the loo, but I am more concerned at the colour of her urine. The white sheet dropped on to the floor is stained an odd colour. I look in the bowl itself and see that the water is thick and brown, and her wee has a pungent, distinctive aroma – like everything else about her.

I clear it all up and wipe over the loo seat.

I find Sky back in her room.

'Sky, do you drink any water?'

'No.'

Her answer doesn't surprise me in the slightest. The glass of water that I left by her bed is untouched. She has drunk fruit juice this morning, and hot chocolate and cola last night. Whenever children come to us, we have to make allowances for the fact that everyone's home life is different, and there is no such thing as 'normal' – but a picture is emerging of what these girls' lives must have been like. Young Sky seems to me as if she has come from another time and place, another world entirely.

And, as ever, I have no one to discuss this all with. I have to wait to hear from the children's new social worker – and when that does happen, it is likely to be a case of me briefing her rather than the other way round. I decide that it would be as well to run my observations by Maz. Even though we are still in the early days and I don't know her very well, I find that I like her more and more.

When I call, she is driving between meetings and has me on speaker.

'Hi, Louise, good to hear from you. I should just say that I'm not alone; I've got a colleague in the car with me. Are you still happy to chat?'

I appreciate her professionalism and honesty. Sometimes in the past it hasn't been this way for us. As foster carers, sometimes we feel as though we're the bottom rung of the ladder and are treated with a total lack of respect, sometimes even contempt.

'No problem. Thanks for letting me know. I just wanted to update you on a few things relating to Sky and Avril.'

Maz is concerned.

'I'll tell you what I'll do. As soon as I get back to the office I'll do some digging to see what's been happening for these girls – and together we'll think through the best way we can support them. It sounds as if there are medical issues here, certainly for Sky, on top of everything else.'

'It would help if we knew who the new social worker was.'

'It would,' she agrees, 'but that doesn't stop us from making a good start. It will put us into a strong position if we know exactly what we think they might need going forward.'

I feel a little more relieved than when I picked up the phone. I'm glad now that I rang. It doesn't exactly feel as though my problem has been halved, but sharing it at least makes me feel as though I'm not trying to do this alone. To be honest, it is Avril's behaviour that bothers me more than Sky's, and the way she seems to be in cahoots with her mother to make life difficult.

I go to see Lloyd, who is busy in his studio. 'Would you like some lunch?'

He looks at his watch. 'Why not?'

Lloyd is probably one of the most laid-back and generous-hearted men I have ever met – which is probably why I married him. After my own childhood abuses, which seemed to segue into making bad choices of boyfriend, almost as a form of self-harm, I was lucky to find Lloyd. He never judges me, is always kind, and somehow lacks the weird ego that might exist between two creative types living together. He never seems to feel the need to be top dog; he is always relaxed, around both professional and private matters. So I am surprised by what he says as he sits down with me to eat.

'Louise, I have a bad feeling about these two.'

He doesn't have a 'bad feeling' bone in him. We have looked after children who have thrown things at Lloyd, hit him, sworn at him – you name it, he has taken it in his stride. He is always able to put it down to their trauma and separate the behaviour from the person. These two haven't done anything remotely on that kind of scale, and yet he is saying this.

'Why?' I ask.

'It's not so much Sky – though she is a strange child. Is she even a child?'

'She doesn't seem to understand much about being a child,' I agree, realising that I have not yet shared some of this morning's observations and the additional things I have picked up about her background. 'She seems to exist in a permanent state of wonder. Things that we take for granted – certainly things that our other children have had – just don't seem to have been part of her experience.' I also understand this on a personal level. I am the first to admit that because of my own childhood, I have a tendency to overcompensate when I encounter certain things that I feel were missing. It's why I can relate to Lily's smell-feast super-sense. I recognise something like this in Sky, and I have a deep desire to help her.

'It's Avril.'

'I know. I have a bad feeling there, too.'

'Now, we know it's wrong to hang anything on a child in care—'

'Deeply wrong.'

'But—'

Before he can expand on the 'but' there are three rapid pings on my phone – which I have left in my bag out in the hall.

'I think I can guess who that might be.'

I bring it in, sit back down and scroll through the texts. They are all from Hanna – and more than just the three notifications I have just heard.

First of all, there are messages from Hanna complaining that she doesn't like the way we are doing certain things. The girls don't like cereal for breakfast. Sky should only travel in the car when absolutely necessary. They both prefer white bread to brown. The one that really gets me is the penultimate one.

Avril wants new trainers.

In the next message, not only has Hanna sent me a picture of the trainers Avril wants, but a price too: £109. Seriously. What is this woman about?

I show Lloyd. After scrolling through the texts he says, without hesitation, 'Block her number.'

I do it, straight away.

We are happy that we have a solution – at least for the time being.

When you foster a child, you also take on their family and extended family. It goes without saying. Yet in all our years of fostering, so far we've only known one family who thanked us for our work and what we did for their child. Nobody comes into this world for the praise, but neither do they for constant demands like this. It is more than a little weird, and I feel so much better when it's done. I realise that I have been avoiding looking at my phone. Her messages really have been getting to me.

We finish our lunch and something about our decision must be troubling me, because I decide to call Maz again and explain.

She has been nothing but sympathetic so far, so I'm surprised – and a little annoyed – when she says, 'Sorry, Louise, but you can't do that. Section 20 means that you need to be available to talk to the parents if they wish. As it's still only day one, we don't have enough evidence to justify blocking her. Can you unblock her, please?'

I am furious, and feel the unfairness of it keenly. I have opened up my house to two children. I don't want this level of interference from a birth parent. It's both petty and calculating. But Maz was very clear, and so I do what she says and unblock Hanna's number.

Almost immediately, there are more texts from Hanna.

'Oh, here we go,' I say. This time I am fuming.

Hi Louise, it's the birth parents' right to know where our children are and to speak to the foster carer if we wish.

How on earth did she know that – and how is it that she has used almost exactly the same language as Maz just has? Does she know, somehow, that I have just been talking to Maz?

I fly out of the room, up the stairs and knock quickly on Avril's door, entering immediately. She is still on her bed, now with the new hoodie on, plugged back into her headphones and playing on her Xbox. She looks at me and smiles. It is a very knowing smile, a smug smile, as though she has won something. Or am I imagining it?

I go back downstairs to Lloyd.

He looks as annoyed as I feel.

'I don't know. She's on her bed. I suppose she could have been listening outside the door and called her mum. I just don't know.'

'Well, now we know something,' Lloyd says. 'We know that we have a spy in the house.'

'What are we going to do?'

'There's nothing we can do – for now. But I don't like it. I don't like it one little bit.'

'Neither do I. And why am I sitting in my own kitchen – in my own kitchen – feeling like this is warfare?'

'I know. That's exactly what it is. I was going to say earlier that it's wrong to blame a child for something, but Avril's behaviour feels threatening.'

Lloyd shoots me a look. It's filled with concern, and something that matches my own feeling. It is close to fear.

It's amazing how quickly your mood and thoughts change when you don't feel safe in your own home. How fragile everything suddenly seems, as if it might all unravel should I pull on a single thread.

Chapter Six

In the afternoon Maz calls back.

'Look, I'm sorry if I sounded a bit sharp earlier, but we have to make sure that we stay within the law.'

I have a few opinions about 'the law' right now, but I bite my tongue.

I walk through the house while I am talking to Maz. It feels better to be pacing, but I am also looking for Sky, who was not in her room as I walked past. Neither is she playing with toys in the sitting room, and I have a sudden panic that she has got out, somehow.

'Bear with me a moment, Maz.'

I walk towards Avril's room, still with the phone against my ear.

Beyond the door I can hear Sky's voice.

I have explained to both girls that if they are in their rooms by themselves they can keep the door shut – but if anyone else is in there they must keep it open or at least ajar. Avril knows this, and yet she has the door firmly shut. Why? I listen.

I hear Sky talking to someone else on the phone, not her sister. I guess that it is probably her mum – which makes the arrangements about contact that need to be discussed with the new social worker pretty pointless.

The anger rises up within me and I surprise myself by how cross I feel. If we must stick to 'the law', then surely

Hanna must too. In closing her door like this, Avril has already broken one of the mandatory safeguarding rules that we have to agree to when we sign up to become foster carers, but that is not what is making me angry. The fury arises from a kind of fear, because I feel like I don't have control in my home. Then, as I listen further, it becomes something more. Something else. Something deeper and darker than that.

I hear Sky say, 'Yes, Mum. Yes, I will. I will do that.' A pause. 'Yes, I hate Louise.'

I walk quickly up the hall into our bedroom and close the door carefully behind me. Maz couldn't hear what was being said, but I relay all the details to her.

She is calm; much calmer than I am. 'Birth parents are usually angry that foster carers have their children, Louise. You can understand that. Some even blame the foster carers for the whole situation.'

I make a 'huh' sound.

'I know that sounds bizarre, but they do.'

I must be taking my frustration out on Maz, because my tone is sarcastic as I hear myself say, 'Oh yes, of course. Because we have the authority to take them directly from their birth family, don't we?'

Maz ignores that, but she has some news.

'I've found out a little bit of information that I think might help to give a bit of context and background.'

'I'm all ears.'

'The girls' parents are both political activists. They both belong to this underground anti-establishment movement called the Stone Ground Group.'

'I've never heard of them.'

'No, neither had I, but I've been doing a bit of research. They're quite radical, pretty hard-core and, as fairly active members, we think it's quite likely that they're being watched by authorities higher than ours: the Home Office. It looks like they've made some big claims about the government. Plenty of anti-government sentiment generally, and some threats.'

I laugh. 'Anti-government sentiment? Sounds like most people in the park or the pub, probably.'

Maz goes on. 'True, but this seems to be a bit more serious than a rant in the park or the pub. The girls' father actually seems to be one of the founders of this group. It looks like they are all intellectuals and academics – but very left-wing.'

I never like to discuss politics with social workers. I think the old stereotype of a vegetarian driving a 2CV with CND stickers in their back window has well and truly disappeared. These days social workers carry briefcases and wear smart suits and sometimes turn up at your door with what I would consider to be some dubious views about funding.

'Interesting,' I say. And my interest is definitely piqued. 'Is there any way I can learn more about this group? What did you say they were called?'

'Stone Ground. There is a website for them, but you sort of have to know how to find it. It doesn't come up straight away in search engines. And anyway, you can't snoop.'

'It's not snooping—' I start to say.

'Foster carers are not allowed to look at birth families on Facebook or on any other social media, as you know.'

Of course Lloyd and I do know – and have cheerfully ignored this many times in the past. Sometimes, without doing a little internet research we'd never have been able to help the police find absconders or defend ourselves from violent uncles who want their niece back for purposes that are often related to the very reason she is in care. So we don't call it snooping. That would suggest that we are nosy – which we aren't. We prefer to call it 'research', to enable us to be informed. The sort of information that might help to create the sense of a child's identity; to foster greater understanding about the child living in our family home. That, and – on rare occasions – to help us know when to seek advice from the police if we need to. In the past, when violent birth-family members have called at our house, we have told the police. After all, this is our family home, and the police are the ones who can deal with these matters directly and effectively. But we aren't even talking about social media in this case.

'If it's a website, in the public domain, that can't count in the same way, can it?'

Maz, who, like most social workers, has to walk a fine line between supporting us, safeguarding the children, protecting herself, and defending the organisation that she works for, says diplomatically, 'Just keep track of everything and write it up in your daily log.'

'I will,' I promise.

I do this meticulously anyway, particularly when we are at the start of a new placement. You have to keep tight daily records. We still have to keep good records even for Lily, who has been with us for more than five years now, though we no longer have to record the fact that she has brushed her hair or eaten her dinner – that would be pretty pointless – but if something significant happens I email her social worker and copy in our supervising social worker immediately. I feel like I could fill pages about Sky and Avril – and Hanna – already. I have to keep reminding myself, as Maz just did, that this is actually still their first full day with us.

I feel fortified after talking to Maz, and knock on Avril's door.

'How are you doing? Would you both like a hot chocolate and biscuit?'

They look towards me and nod. In fact, Sky is off the bed and on her way downstairs before I have the chance to finish talking.

I say to Avril, 'As you know already, I need you to have your door open if someone else is in the room with you. We all have to abide by this rule – it's not mine, but one that is enforced by the local authority.'

She looks at me with her smug, but-what-could-I-possibly-be-doing-wrong expression. 'Okay.'

She follows me downstairs where I make them hot chocolate. Sky says 'thank you', but Avril hardly speaks.

I watch her as she places her iPhone on to her lap surreptitiously, almost – as if it's a secret. I find myself assuming that she is recording us – and begin talking in a slightly artificial way – in my best impression of the model foster carer. For an audience. For Hanna.

I will do this by the book. I will do this in a way that means she will struggle to find fault with anything I say or do.

I also acknowledge to myself at the same time that the whole thing is madness. How long will it go on for? How can we possibly live like this every day?

Chapter Seven

When the girls go back upstairs it feels like a tiny victory that Avril keeps the door open – even if it is to the distance of about two inches. I am pleased to feel that I have regained some control in my home.

Lloyd is busy working on a logo for a client, but not too busy that he can't be interrupted for this latest update. I explain about the girls' parents belonging to this political group.

He rolls his eyes and goes to Google. He taps in the name – nothing comes up in the first few pages. He adds some keywords – and there it is.

There is not much to go on at first glance. The home page shows a side-view image of an open laptop at a desk with a dark-grey-toned background. Much of the site is on a black background.

Lloyd, with his graphic designer goggles on, reacts. 'Oh dear. White type on black – not good.'

'I think the font colours are the least of our worries.' I lean in and start reading the contents. There is an 'about' page. I discover that the group was formed in the nineties at a polytechnic in the north of England. There is a photo of a bunch of what looks like lecturers and students. Underneath is a list of names: John Wiseman, an economist. That rings a bell. I am sure his name was on the referral. I go and get it from my locked cabinet in our office. The girls' surname is not Wiseman but Hopfgarten. I wonder if part of the ethos of Stone Ground is that the child inherits the mother's name. That could be seen as radical in some camps. There is a similarity in features. John Wiseman must be Avril's dad. I wonder if he is Sky's dad, but with all the extra flesh around Sky's face it is hard to distinguish her features, yet alone compare them to John Wiseman's.

I read more of the political content on the site, and, in some ways at least, find myself agreeing with what Stone Ground is saying. They talk about the dismantling of a capitalist system that is making money and profit from the blood and sweat of workers who have no rights. As a foster carer who watches children's social care becoming privatised and resources gradually disappearing, I can relate to some of this. I read on. It's a bit too intellectual for my little brain, but I get the gist and agree with much of the principle, until they talk about acts of sabotage – primarily digital sabotage, and using computer hacking as a protest tool to bring down corporate control. So that's why there's a picture of a laptop on the home page.

My thoughts turn quickly to Hanna, and I wonder if somehow she or Avril have not just accessed my phone to find my number, but actually hacked into it somehow. It's a scary thought that would have seemed far-fetched a few hours ago. Less so now. I go back into the office and look at my own laptop. I wonder if it's a little open window into my world. When it's not in use, I resolve to keep it in the lockable cupboard. Lloyd hasn't got anything to do with the children and fostering on his work computer; it's all on my laptop.

Lloyd's declaration that we had a spy in the house seemed fanciful, but now I try to adjust my thinking to the fact that he is very likely right, and we are indeed being spied upon. I feel threatened, amongst many other things, but maybe this is how it works. This must be how they do their corporate bullying. Except that I am not a big corporation – I'm just me.

I go back to Lloyd and discover him adding an additional layer of security to his work computer. He is thinking along exactly the same lines as me. We have suddenly become mindful of all our devices. I do a quick inventory. The other children have phones, iPads and gaming devices. There are suddenly multiple ways into our home, and I don't know how to lock everything down.

I have another sudden rush of anger. This is just not fair.

I call Maz again and explain my theory now that I've had a chance to look at the Stone Ground website. I detect something of a patronising tone in her voice.

'Don't you think you might be over-reacting, Louise? Just a little bit? Hacking? Really? The girl is 14 years old. That's quite a serious accusation.'

'I don't know that it's Avril. I think she's probably acting under her mother's direction. I know that they're in pretty much constant communication. And Hanna knows things she just shouldn't know. She used your exact words about rights, just seconds after you did!'

'Louise, they weren't just my words. They're in the guidelines for the Section 20. Which are freely available online, and more than likely in the documentation that the Wiseman-Hopfgartens were given. You're being paranoid.'

'Ah, so it is Wiseman.'

'Sorry?'

'Nothing. Just identifying names with faces on the website.'

'Louise—'

'I haven't looked at any social media.'

'No, but perhaps I shouldn't have told you about the Stone Ground website.'

'I'm glad you did. It's already helped to explain a few things.'

She reminds me that we can't prove anything and assures me, in her social-workery way, that everything will be all right.

'We just need to give it time to settle,' she finishes.

I love it when social workers use the royal 'we' when they talk about behaviour issues of foster children in the home – when they don't live there or have to deal with it themselves.

Before we know it, the other children are back home. Hungry and thirsty, they begin to do their daily after-school raid of the kitchen. These days I have this off to a fine art. In supermarkets they have loss leaders, items that are deliberately placed to catch the eye but also to encourage the purchase of more expensive items. I follow this principle. In my kitchen, I place food that is attractive but not too filling. Snacks that will not ruin their dinner, but will keep them going and make them feel that they have some sort of treat.

Sky begins to make her way downstairs as she hears all the noise and commotion. She is gaining a little confidence and greater mobility as she tackles them, but I still rush to be in front of her just in case she slips or falls. Every single time I see Sky she is beaming. She looks so happy, as though the smile is permanently stitched on to her face.

I've also noticed that, unlike nearly all our other foster children, she hasn't asked one question about her parents. In fact, she hasn't mentioned them at all as far as I can recall. It's unusual, but perhaps not altogether surprising, given that I know she has definitely spoken to her mother on the phone at least once. If I hurry, I can catch Maz before she leaves for home. As it's Friday, I'm sure she won't be hanging about. I catch her just as she is heading for her car.

'Yes, sorry. It's me again. I know it feels like I'm phoning you non-stop, but things keep coming up. I forgot to mention earlier, but I thought you should know that Sky is talking to her parents on the phone whenever she feels like it.'

'Ah.' Maz is silent for a moment. 'Well, that rather makes a mockery of supervised contact – if they are already talking on the telephone unsupervised.'

'Exactly my thought.'

'Bloody phones. I hate them. They're the root cause of most of my problems with children. Every single day.'

'I'm not surprised. Is there a policy or any guidance I can look at?'

To my surprise Maz spits a bitter laugh. 'No. No policy. Don't be daft – of course not. We have to figure out each issue as it comes, think on our feet and hope that we get it right.'

'Okay,' I say. 'So what about in this case? What do we do about the girls talking to their parents?'

'Look, I know that it was noted for the care plan that Avril and Sky should only have supervised contact – which means there are issues of concern. But Louise, the reality is that we can't stop Avril speaking to her parents on a phone that they have paid for. It's Avril's property.'

'Blimey, Maz. Just tell me what the hell we're meant to do. Hanna's banging on about her rights. What about mine?'

'I don't know. I really don't. If I'm honest, I haven't got a clue. For now we just have to keep an eye on it. Then see if the new social worker has any ideas. He or she will have a view, I'm sure.'

In this moment, I am convinced that fostering is a form of madness.

Thankfully the feeling passes as I notice Sky in the kitchen, talking to the other children. Lily, who is always keen to be helpful, seems to be a little more at ease with Sky, but I watch my sons all at sea, not quite knowing what to say to her. She is a strange construct. She's not just a little bit chubby, she's enormously swollen and expanded, and she can't walk properly. It's a challenge to look at her ball-shaped face with only indentations for eyes and mouth, and a nose that hardly protrudes from it. They have never seen anyone who looks like this before. But it isn't just her looks, it's her actions, too. She is behaving like the dogs when there is food around – staring at the children and their snacks.

I walk up to Sky and offer her a banana. She looks at me quizzically.

'Have you eaten one before?'

She shakes her head.

'Do you know what I mean by a banana?'

She nods. 'I saw it in a counting book that had a picture of a monkey eating one.'

I realise then that Sky is sharp. She has so little life experience, but she is taking the information that she receives from books and television and storing it up carefully. I realise that I don't know if she can read or write. I have made the assumption that she can't, because of the schooling issues, but perhaps I am jumping to the wrong conclusions.

Lily takes a banana from the fruit bowl and shows Sky how to peel it.

Sky seems to think this is amazing. She couldn't grin any harder if she tried, I'm sure. She eats the banana and announces, 'This is amazing.'

I know that she has a sweet tooth, but perhaps I can start to encourage her to eat more fruit instead of biscuits. I suggest that all the children have a glass of water.

The boys look at me as though I have just asked them to drink from the dogs' bowl. They would usually tuck into squash after school. I give them the look that attempts to communicate an earnest *Please help me out here.*

Jackson frowns but gets four cups from the cupboard. He fills each one up and passes it to a child. Sky is engrossed in watching everything Jackson does. I swoop in to both Lily and Vincent and whisper, 'We need to get Sky to drink water.'

They both look at me and nod.

'Wow, thanks Jackson. This water is *so* lovely,' says Vincent.

Lily joins in. 'Mmmm. I love water. It's so refreshing.'

I love them so much for seizing the moment for me, but I don't want them to overdo it. We're going to start sounding like an advert for Evian if we're not careful.

My phone pings: a sound that previously would have made me rush over to see whom the notification was from, but now fills me with dread because I *know* who it will be.

I'm not wrong. It is another text from Hanna.

I would appreciate it if you didn't interfere with my daughter's health.

Wow. Now that's mad.

Almost without thinking, I text back. *It's my job to help support your children to understand that eating and living healthily is good for them.*

Straight away another text message comes in. She evidently has the nimble fingers and thumbs of a teenager.

It's their right to live their lives how they want.

I wait then, and choose not to respond, a little bit cross with myself for reacting to the first one. I think – no, more than think, I *know* – that somehow she is watching us or has some kind of surveillance in operation in the kitchen. How can she not?

'Come on, children. Let's go and see what's on television,' I say. I just want to be out of this room.

Jackson needs no further invitation and disappears immediately to his room to game. After a while of sitting with them, I stand up to leave the younger children in the sitting room watching the television. I remember that I must find a way to get Sky to give me those toxic knickers that she seems so reluctant to relinquish. After a short period of respite, the smell is coming back through the clean clothes. Lily politely displays no outward sign of being bothered by the odour, but Vincent is looking a little uncomfortable.

'Can I go in the garden for a bit?' he asks, wrinkling up his nose so that I guess the reason for his escape attempt.

'Of course. Are you two going to carry on watching?' I ask the girls, who nod, engrossed in an episode of *Octonauts*. Captain Barnacles has just sounded the octo-alert, so things are hotting up.

I wander upstairs to find Jackson leaning into Avril's room, holding his controller for his PlayStation. He and Avril are discussing the respective merits of Xbox and PlayStation consoles. I think this is a good sign and smile at Jackson – who ignores me.

I go back downstairs to update Lloyd, who has a grim expression on his face.

'You're not going to like this,' he says. He has Hanna's Facebook page up on his screen where, to my horror, she has posted a picture of our bedroom.

Chapter Eight

Though my instinct is to rush upstairs and confront Avril – how else could Hanna have obtained such a private image of our personal space? – Lloyd persuades me not to say anything to her at all. He's right. Avril doesn't need to know that we have looked at her mum's Facebook; in fact, because we aren't technically allowed to look at their social media, I shouldn't say anything. I clearly can't say anything to Maz either, which is frustrating.

This is such a strange feeling. I'm used to being able to defend myself, but this situation is so unfamiliar; a bit like 'quietly' being in a fight – but with a woman I have never even met, and who has never actually met me. She was taken to court because she was neglecting her children, and now those children are with us. I can see why there might be resentment, but it's not my fault, and I genuinely don't feel safe in my home now. In fact, I feel vulnerable. But that's exactly why she's doing it. John Wiseman's political group does this to disrupt the corporate state, to cause as much mischief as possible, but we are not the corporate state. We're just foster carers who happen to have said yes to a referral for two children. It feels unfair.

Over the next few hours Hanna continues to send messages.

Sky would like a biscuit.
Avril wants an energy drink.

Sky's room is too cold.

Avril needs another blanket on her bed.

Sky does not wish to take a bath tonight.

Avril would like to be woken later in the morning.

Sky would like hamburgers for dinner tomorrow.

Avril doesn't like lasagne.

Sky doesn't want to do PE at school tomorrow.

I ignore each text. Though I can't help but raise an eyebrow at 'hamburgers', plural.

She calls to speak to me a few times, but I ignore her.

Meanwhile, Sky is dealing with her own private little battle. At bedtime she asks if she can sleep in her new coat.

'Well, I think you might be too hot if you wear that in bed', I say. 'It's much thicker than your other one.'

'Can I wear the other one then?'

'Ah, that's still drying from the wash', I say, though the truth is that I haven't brought it in from the washing line yet. Sky's peculiar 'perfume' seems to be ingrained in the very fabric of it, and I can't bear it in the house. I also can't get rid of it permanently, as technically it belongs to Hanna and it simply isn't my place to make that (sensible) decision.

She looks sad, and I remember that the new coat is a mini-breakthrough. I don't want to do anything that will destroy our little win.

'Look, I tell you what. If you wear your pyjamas and get into bed, we could lay your new one on top, like a blanket.'

Parenting is ever the exercise in compromise and negotiation.

I'll remove it when she's asleep.

We spend the next few days tiptoeing through our home, trying to test out which areas of the house might be less risky to relax in, under less surveillance. I find myself searching in corners of the kitchen to see if I can discover some kind of hidden camera or recording device. When I find nothing at all I wonder if I've completely lost the plot. Am I going mad? Lloyd evidently wonders the same thing when he finds me unscrewing the back of the microwave.

'Louise, what the hell are you doing?'

I'm not sure I even know the answer. It really does feel like mind games.

But Hanna is clever and, even though I am trying not to answer her, she manages to catch me off guard at times.

I'm out shopping locally when my mobile goes and the display shows a number I don't recognise – not Hanna's. It could be anyone. The nature of my work means that I am usually expecting a call from someone – either about my books or paintings or something in between.

But it is Hanna – evidently using a different phone or SIM.

'Hi, Louise. I just want to see how my children are.'

She doesn't say, 'as is my right', but I can hear it in her tone.

'They are fine. Doing well. How are you?'

She seems a little taken aback by my question.

'Oh. Yes. I'm fine, thanks.'

'That's great. Bye then,' I say, and block the number as I hang up. I feel that I can block this one with impunity because Hanna's is the other number that I have already saved. It occurs to me that maybe this is John's phone, but I can legitimately claim not to know that.

While I wrestle with my paranoia that every word I speak is being overheard, and dodge calls and messages from Hanna, over that first week we do make some progress in other areas, albeit in small steps. At dinnertime Avril finally begins to come downstairs and seems happy to sit and eat her food with us, and make conversation with Jackson about gaming. Avril and Jackson get on fine if the subject is gaming; it's a topic that has become a way for Avril to experiment with conversation and the beginning of social cohesion. It results in a sort of stilted polite conversation, and it reinforces my sense that Avril and Sky can't have had much, or indeed perhaps *any* social interaction. Being with other people is new to them, but I have a strong belief in the theory that humans are instinctively social animals and thrive on being together. I hope that my theory will prove to be correct in this case.

I get the sense that although Avril is probably disobeying Hanna by joining us for evening meals, she is now at least a little happier to be with us than she was in the first 24 hours of her stay. I don't particularly trust her any more than I did, but her manner is less strange and cold and perhaps, if I'm completely honest, she is almost veering the other way now. She is in our personal space, and both girls have very little concept of personal space. The other children, including Lily, do. They seem to instinctively create a healthy space between themselves and whomever they talk to – unless going in for a hug. But I notice that neither Avril nor Sky seems to have a clue. When they are interacting with us they are *way* too close. I find it uncomfortable, but now that Avril is finally beginning to make more of an effort to interact with us generally, I feel reluctant to bring it up in case I unintentionally interfere with this progress. I wonder if I should gently ask them to move back an inch or two, but it's difficult to know how to raise the whole thing. I have had the unnerving experience of standing in the kitchen assuming that I am by myself, only to turn round and find

101

Avril standing right there. She is like a ghost, and startles me when she suddenly appears and disappears almost soundlessly in unexpected places.

I have washed Sky's coat three times now and it still smells. There is no way I can think of to get rid of the grease marks. I tell Maz that I want to throw it out, but she gets a little shirty with me and reminds me that as it's the property of the children's mother I will need to bag it up and get it back to her. I know this, but it reveals more systemic stupidity as far as I am concerned, since I would have to drive for over an hour – and walk to the door of the home of the birth family. According to the guidelines I'm not meant to meet them – neither am I supposed to know where they live – so it doesn't feel like the soundest advice on offer. All I know is that I don't want the bloody thing in my house.

'Why don't you post it back to Hanna?' Lloyd suggests.

That seems like a good idea until I discover that this will cost £12 – and again, I would have to know their address. I put it inside two bags and 'file it' in the back of her wardrobe for the time being. It's definitely not hidden at all. If you looked really hard, right at the back, you'd find it.

I decide not to mention it again. There are some conversations that really are not worth having with a social worker. When Lloyd gets the fire bin out to burn his old paperwork a few days later, I pull it out from the back of her wardrobe and it has an unceremonious cremation. For a while I worry that I'll get into trouble, but Sky never asks for it, thankfully. I don't fancy explaining that one to Hanna.

Lloyd continues to check Hanna's Facebook page. She seems to have gone quiet, and at least that invasion of personal space doesn't seem to develop. No more pictures of our bedroom appear.

It's day nine in the Big Brother household – or at least it might as well be, given how constantly 'watched' I feel. I've already learnt not to assume anything about Sky's awareness of food. She is busy helping me to clean out the kitchen cupboards, when, right at the back of them, we discover the boys' old egg cups. Jackson's is a black-and-white cow, and Vincent's is shaped as a pink pig. For some reason he was bats about pigs when he was little, but it's years since they've used them.

Sky seems to think they are amazing.

'Have you ever used one of these before?'

A shake of the head.

'Would you like to try a boiled egg? With some soldiers to dip in the egg?'

She raises an eyebrow, looking at me as if she is worried that I am disturbed.

I boil the egg – a little longer than I would like to if I was cooking it for myself. I make the decision not to give her a runny egg. Some children are funny about the consistency of food, and I don't want to disturb her. It isn't quite hard-boiled, still a little bit gooey in the middle when I serve it up to her. I head to the bread bin only to find that it's empty. The locusts have been through: the older children seem to be on an eating cycle of every half hour at the moment. Bread doesn't last five minutes amidst hollow legs and massive growth spurts. I find and toast the last bagel, and after slathering it with delicious salted butter, I cut it into strips. I place the little meal on the table.

'Come and sit down, Sky.'

She is wide-eyed and excited at this new adventure – eager to get going. I turn away to tidy up, and when I turn back to chat and to see how she is getting on, she is holding a near-naked white soft egg with a spoon stuck in its side, ripping it apart with her hands.

My fault. I have not explained. I take a deep intake of breath and place the remaining shelled end in the egg cup. It is too wobbly to scoop with bagel toast. So, I resort to plan B and show her how to eat it with one hand.

'Eat it a bit like an apple,' I suggest.

I launch into my standard explanation about how important manners are – and how throughout life we are judged kindly and cruelly for our standards of manners.

'Our manners tell the world a lot about who we are and what we want.'

I don't think she's listening. She loves the taste of that egg and I resolve to buy in extra and add them to the morning breakfast menu. Sometimes it's easy to overlook the obvious delights in life that some children in care have never experienced.

The smell that emanates from Sky is less offensive than when she first arrived, and the really awful note that I thought was dirty knickers has faded somewhat. But it is still not nice to be around her directly. As if I needed any other indicator, the dogs keep reminding me. They make a beeline to sniff her crotch and nose around her body. When she lies down on the floor they both snuffle into her head. She thinks this is funny and starts laughing, but I think it's sad, and won't stop until we get her properly clean. Her hair is greasy and retains the taint of tobacco smoke, as well as just the general pervasive aroma of poor hygiene. I have tried running more baths for her, but the pattern repeats where she pretends to have got into the tub, but I know she hasn't actually been near the water. Whatever happens, I must get some soap on to her hair – by fair means or foul.

I have a quiet word with Lily, explaining that if she goes along with my plan and we are successful then there is a new pair of leggings in it for her. She's more than happy to oblige, and I'll deal later with the fact that I have once again resorted to bribery in my parenting life.

My master plan is to undertake a 'performance' of washing Lily's hair in the kitchen sink. First we set up the salon with towels and a shower hose from the bathroom. Then I set out the products: strawberry and citrus fruit-flavoured shampoos, hair masks that smell amazing, conditioner, mousse, combs and brushes. I play some music in the background to turn it into a little bit of a spa party.

'Is madam ready to take her seat?' I say, offering Lily a chair stacked up with coloured cushions that I have to help lift her on to.

Sky watches close by and while I am wetting down Lily's hair she breathes in every detail.

'Is the water hot or cold?'

'Hmm. Lovely and warm,' Lily replies.

'Does it hurt?'

Lily answers first with a dreamy smile, then says that it feels wonderful.

I hold the open bottles up to Sky so that she can take in the scents.

'Mmmm. Can I eat some?' she asks, sniffing.

Lily and I laugh, and Sky joins in with the laughter, beaming away.

I spend time massaging Lily's scalp.

'Oh, that feels so nice. I could enjoy this all day long,' she says. 'It's like heaven.'

Just as with the water drinking, I start to wonder if we might be overdoing it, when Sky says, 'Can you wash my hair, Louise?'

'Sure, if you would like that.' Inside I'm singing and dancing and air-punching.

She nods her head enthusiastically and picks up a towel to drape around her shoulders, copying Lily.

I send Lily upstairs to get the hairdryer. Meanwhile I get Sky into the salon chair. It is not nearly so easy to manoeuvre around her body and reach the taps to get the water temperature right.

'How does that feel? Not too hot?'

'It's fine.'

I gently massage foamy shampoo into her knotted, dirty hair, and feel great. I have wanted to do that for days. I rinse and repeat several times, constantly checking that she likes it, that the water feels OK, that no suds go anywhere near her eyes.

'Shall we try some coconut conditioner?' I ask.

'Hmmm.'

Conditioner will help with the knots, I hope.

After I have rinsed her head for a final time I gently pat her hair to dry it off, then use the towel to make a turban. I hold up the hand mirror so that she can see her reflection.

She gives a little scream of joy.

I leave her sitting with a glass of water. She chats away like a bird that has found her song, and keeps holding up the mirror to steal another look at herself.

I dry Lily's hair with a rounded brush and hairdryer, giving her the full salon treatment. She has beautiful long dark hair with a lustrous sheen to it. It looks fantastic. I'm very proud of her hair. When she first arrived with us several years ago it was in a right state – not quite to Sky's levels, but after the many visits to the hairdressers that have happened since, it is now very much her crowning glory.

I walk back over to Sky, who sits bright-eyed with expectation. I gently hold her hair and begin teasing the knots. I'm mindful that I don't pull her hair, and wonder if scissors to cut out some of the worst ones might be a kinder option.

'Does this feel okay?' I ask.

'Yes.'

There is a pause while I work away at a stubborn tangle.

Suddenly, she says, 'Hanna hurt my hair. She burnt my head with the water and hit me with the brush.'

Oh, this poor child. No wonder she has been reluctant to have her hair interfered with. No wonder she preferred to leave it in that horrible, dreadlocked state rather than suffer that kind of physical abuse. I make a mental note to pass this information on to the social worker.

I remember that she was calling her mother 'Hanna' when speaking with her on the phone the other day, too. I know there are plenty of families who prefer first names and don't use the familial titles of Mummy, Mum, Mama – or another variation, but it seems another signal of the way that Sky is so peculiarly grown-up in certain aspects of her life. A thought strikes me suddenly. Even though my instinct is to use 'Mummy', I follow her lead.

'Did Hanna wash your hair in the bath?'

Sky nods, and frowns.

That may explain why she resists getting into the bath. But then I remember the odd comment she made about sleeping in the bath and it being full up.

'How long has your old bath been full up so you can't sleep in it?'

She makes a thinking face. 'Twenty years.'

I laugh. But judging by the grime in Sky's hair, I would guess it is a significant amount of time. I spend an entire hour gently combing her hair, teasing away at the tangles as much as I dare. Lily stays in the kitchen and the two of them chat away.

When we are done, she doesn't exactly look as though she has just stepped out of a salon. Like the clothes that needed several goes around the washing machine, her hair still smells – and there are still plenty of matted knots and stubborn clumps – but I feel happy.

We did something big today.

Chapter Nine

At last we get a call from the girls' new social worker. He introduces himself as Charles, and explains that he wants to come and visit the girls, and us, as soon as possible. I am pleased, of course, but also feel protective towards Avril and Sky at the thought of the stress of having to meet yet another adult responsible for making big decisions about their lives. Any foster carer will tell you how protective of the children in your care you become. These girls, strange as they are, need protecting all the more.

He sounds all right on the phone, but it's hard to tell. I hope he *will* turn out to be all right. I do a call round to my fellow foster carers to ask if anyone knows anything about him, but get very little back. It looks like he's new, probably a locum.

At dinner I tell the girls that next week after school they will meet Charles. 'Which is a great step forward,' I finish.

Avril makes a face and disappears behind her hair and under her hoodie. Since she's been here she has showered every day without prompting. I've managed to get some more new clothes for her, ordered online. She just will not go out shopping with me. She doesn't seem to like being outside very much at all. She's gone to school all week but says that she hates it. She hasn't asked to go anywhere or to meet any friends. Actually, I'm not sure if she even has any friends. Life is difficult when you come from the kind of disruption she has: when school itself, in all likelihood, is perceived as one of the institutions that need bringing down. But it's still early days, and it isn't easy to make friends at Avril's age when students have already been attending secondary school for a few years and friendships are firmly established. I know that Sky hasn't, because it is easier to speak to her teacher for a brief word at the end of the school day. In Sky's case, not only has she not been there long enough to make friends, but there is the additional barrier of the way she looks.

After dinner they retreat upstairs, and when I go past Avril's room I notice that the door is shut and Sky is in there with her. I can hear her little voice. I'm annoyed again. I thought we had been through this one and successfully established the ground rules, but it seems not. Before I knock, I hear Sky's voice again.

'Okay, Mum. Sorry, I mean Hanna.'

She's on the phone, and it definitely sounds as if her mother doesn't like being called 'mum', but prefers her first name. It's another little insight towards understanding more about the way Hanna has been parenting the girls. What I find fascinating is that there is hardly any mention of John Wiseman. To the best of my knowledge they are still together as a couple, and his disability makes him housebound, I believe, so he must be there the whole time. Interesting that he seems not to feature. I don't think I've heard either of the girls talk about him at all.

I knock sharply and open the door.

'Time to get your pyjamas on, Sky,' I say, breezily.

She moans. 'O-oh. But I want to watch Avril game.'

'If you get undressed and ready for bed you can come back in for half an hour – but the door needs to be open.'

'No!' Avril spits. 'It's my room, my space, and I want the door shut!'

I realise that they are very likely still on the phone to Hanna, so I choose my words carefully and enunciate them clearly. 'It's actually *our* room and you are staying in it at our invitation. The room is in our house, and, Avril, as you already know, we need to keep doors open whenever there is someone else in the room. That's just the way it is. We all have to abide by this rule.'

I notice that Avril glances at her phone, confirming my suspicions that Hanna is still listening in. 'So, come along then, Sky,' I say, pointing in the direction of her room and placing my hand on her shoulder to guide her through the door.

She behaves in a way that is quite unlike how she has been before, pushing back against my hand to register her strong resistance. She starts shouting at me, 'Leave me alone. Get off me.'

Avril, too, joins in loudly. 'Yeah, leave her alone. Get your hands off her. Who do you think you are?'

Lloyd appears at the bottom of the stairs. 'What's all the noise? What's going on up there?'

Sky whips herself up into a state and begins screaming. She keeps yelling, 'Get off me, you're hurting me!' I jump backwards at her uncharacteristic reaction, and I am now nowhere near her – though the flailing performance as if she is being beaten continues.

Lloyd has made it to the top of the stairs and stands next to me. Together we watch this strange little girl throw herself around the landing, screaming like a banshee.

'Get off me, get off me!' she cries over and over again.

I don't know what to do. Her behaviour is so unexpected and so peculiar that I am rooted to the spot in shock.

By now the other children have run into the hallway to see what all the commotion is, so now there are five of us watching this bizarre, whirling spectacle.

'Go downstairs,' I tell them. 'Just stay out of the way for a moment. Leave us to sort this out.'

I turn back to see Avril standing half out of her room, holding her phone up and pointing it at us while Sky is in full swing. It is like watching someone possessed with a demon spirit, and it has blown up from nowhere.

But I have a horrible, sick feeling that the whole moment has been carefully crafted. Hanna has somehow orchestrated this to get both Lloyd and me into trouble.

And boy, is there trouble.

Chapter Ten

Within 20 minutes of Sky screaming and shouting and bashing about there is an aggressive knock at the door. Lloyd follows me with a raised eyebrow. Two male uniformed police officers are standing on the doorstep.

'Are you Lloyd and Louise Allen?' the one on the right asks.

'Yes.'

They march in, demanding to see Sky and Avril.

Our other children come running out again to see what is going on. Our house hasn't seen drama like this in a while.

The other officer greets the children.

'Mrs Allen, do you mind if I talk to them?'

I am, frankly, bewildered by the turn events have taken in my house, and say, 'Of course, yes, go ahead,' without thinking about it.

I don't have time to process quite what might be going on here, and consider what might be the best thing to do. I certainly don't stop to consider whether we might, in fact, need a solicitor. To add to the chaos, my mobile goes. It's the 'out of hours' desk at social services informing me that a serious allegation has been made against me directly and advising that the police are on their way.

'Thanks for the warning,' I mutter.

'And of course we'll send two social workers round.'

'Of course.'

I feel hot and confused, and wonder whether I am, in fact, in the middle of some sort of nightmare. How can this actually be happening?

Lloyd looks like thunder, and in the same instant we come to the same conclusion: that Hanna has set us up. She is punishing us for the fact that her children have been removed from her care.

My phone goes again. Frankly, it wouldn't surprise me if it was Dr Who on the line. In reality, it's Maz. She is also on her way as she has just had the call from the out of hours manager. The doorbell rings again. It's like Piccadilly Circus. Suddenly inside our house are more strangers: a man and woman.

The man says, 'I'm Charles, but please call me Charlie. We spoke on the phone earlier? I wasn't expecting to meet you quite so soon,' he says grimly as he walks past me into the melee. The woman with him introduces herself.

'I'm Claire. Charlie's manager.'

Her coat is over her arm as though she has made herself at home already. She wears multiple silver chinking bangles on both arms, and it brings to mind medieval plate armour, as if she is going into battle. I also detect a whiff of cigarettes about her as she brushes past without invitation.

And just like that, our home is not ours. We are suspects. Our children are being interviewed about us – their parents – and the possible ways we might have mistreated them.

I have begun to gather my wits about me, and my initial shock is being replaced by fury.

Hanna knows precisely what she is doing. She wants her children – and ours, probably – removed. That way I will know how she feels, feel the same invasion.

I'm still in the hallway and don't quite know where to put myself.

One policeman has the three children in the sitting room, while the other has gone upstairs, presumably to locate Avril and Sky.

Dotty is angrily barking at Claire and Charlie.

'Um, Louise,' Charlie calls. 'Could you possibly sort out this dog?'

Claire says, in a tone that shrivels me, 'Is this dog dangerous? Call it off!'

Dotty? Dangerous? Oh my God! I don't know whether to laugh or cry. Our world is falling apart before our eyes. I've somehow given permission for strangers to question my children about something we haven't done, and now my dog is being categorised as dangerous. Social workers have the power to demand that a foster carer has their dog destroyed if they deem it to be threatening. Dotty, my oh-so-accurate reader of people, really doesn't like these strangers in our home and is going berserk. She is doing her best to protect her mistress while these strangers are invading our private space and destroying us.

I grab Dotty under one arm and Douglas under the other and bundle them out into the garden.

I run back into the kitchen, fling open a cupboard door and do a silent scream into it.

'Mrs Allen, are you quite all right?' Charlie asks, having followed me into the room, uninvited.

'No. No, I'm not. I'm not "all right" at all,' I thunder. 'In fact, things are very wrong. This is all wrong.'

'I think we all need to sit down,' Lloyd says.

The dogs continue their barking outside – if anything, stepping up the urgency.

Claire stands in front of me. 'I want you to explain exactly what has happened and why you have hurt Sky.'

'I have not touched Sky,' I say, but I hear myself sounding defensive and a little deranged and know that whatever I say to this horrible woman, I am just going to sound like I'm guilty.

'Louise, don't say anything else. Call the union,' Lloyd commands.

Lloyd and I joined the foster care workers' union (the NUPFC) a while back – for support and legal advice were it ever to be needed. As foster carers, we have very few rights and we know from past experience that some social workers and managers can abuse their power and authority. But I don't think either of us ever envisaged a moment quite like this.

I pick up my phone to ring the number and see a message from Hanna.

Now you know what it feels like.

Chapter Eleven

I read the message out to Claire and Charlie. 'She's bloody well done this on purpose. Look. "Now you know what it feels like." It's a set-up, entirely calculated on her part.'

Claire, to whom I have taken an instant dislike, holds out her hand, bangles clinking away up her arm. 'Can I see that?'

I hold it up to her so that she can view the screen, but do not give her the phone.

She clears her throat. 'We're here because we received a call from Hanna Hopfgarten, the girls' mother, a short while ago. She was in hysterics, crying and begging for us to come and get their daughters. She played an audio recording of Sky screaming for you to stop hurting her.'

She reaches for her own phone and plays back that bewildering scene of Sky screaming at and repeatedly calling out, 'Get off me.'

At that moment, the children begin piling back into the kitchen, too. They seem relaxed and calm, not at all perturbed by the strange night and whatever questions they have just been subjected to.

The first police officer follows in behind them. 'Thank you, Mrs Allen, for being so co-operative. And thank you to this lot for their most eloquent answers.'

For a moment, I have an irrational panic about exactly what they might have said. I ask him.

'Ha. No need to worry, Mrs Allen. They all said the same thing: that they heard Sky shouting and screaming, and found you and Lloyd at the top of the stairs, away from Sky, while she did what she did. I've heard the recording that Avril made and of course, as you know, we have to take these things seriously – but so far the children have all stated that neither of you were anywhere near Sky when the recording was made.'

Finally some sense. I'm proud of them for taking everything in their stride and not being panicked by uniformed officers in their house. His colleague arrives in the kitchen just as the doorbell goes again. 'I'm very sorry to have disturbed your evening,' police officer number two says, as Lloyd gets up and goes to let in Maz. 'What a bizarre set of circumstances.'

'You're telling me,' I say, wearily.

Claire and Charlie finally sit down and drop a little of the intimidation act. Now that the truth is unfolding, I also feel far more confident. Maz's arrival helps to confirm our 'innocence', as she calmly relays all the concerns I've been sharing with her about the children and Hanna, and have carefully documented. I show the police officers Hanna's latest text.

The second policeman, the one who was with Avril and Sky, continues in a far more conciliatory tone than when they were first at the door.

'Avril's account didn't add up,' he explains. 'And when I spoke separately to Sky and asked her where Louise hurt her, she immediately told me that she hadn't. "No. Louise didn't hurt me." I can see that we've walked into something a little more complex than we anticipated.'

'I suggest that you block Hanna on your phone,' the first policeman suggests.

Claire gives him a withering look and pipes up. 'No, I'm afraid she can't do that. The children are on a Section 20, so the birth family have to know where the children are.'

'The birth family *know* where we are,' I say, feeling like I'm going round in circles.

'True. And Hanna doesn't need to be able to speak to the foster carers directly, does she?' Officer Two agrees.

Claire doesn't. 'I want these parents to be able to speak to Louise as and when they need to. We have had to do a lot of work with these parents to allow the girls to come into care voluntarily. I want lines of communication open.'

I'm feeling bolder by the minute. 'No. That's not right. I don't want to talk to her – especially after this. Why should I have to?'

I have to try so hard to stop myself reacting to what she says next.

'You are a foster carer and you will do as you are told.'

'I will *what*—?' the rage bubbles up inside me, even though I know that now is really not the moment to get angry.

The two policemen look at each other. Officer One says, 'As far as we are concerned, Mr and Mrs Allen have not done anything to hurt Sky.'

'From what we've seen tonight it would appear that there is indeed some malicious intent behind the call-out,' his partner says.

But Claire isn't finished. 'Though this is not the first complaint against these carers.'

Lloyd and I look at each other in amazement.

'These parents have made other complaints about the care of their children in this house.'

I notice that Maz says nothing. I'm confused.

'Do you know anything about this, Maz?'

She shakes her head and looks serious.

I hoped that we were getting somewhere and sorting things out this evening. But perhaps this is just the start. Hanna is clever, and so is John Wiseman. They are playing us to get their revenge against the authorities who took their children.

Maz chooses this moment to make what seems like a casual enquiry as to whether or not Charlie and Claire have seen the children.

Claire at least has the decency to look a little sheepish, given that the children are supposed to be the reason they are here in the first place.

'No, not yet. They're next.'

Perhaps if they had spent a little less time threatening us, they might have remembered them sooner. They shuffle off through the house, but the policemen remain.

Officer One says, 'Do you remember me?'

I look at him more closely. Up until now he has just been a strange policeman in a uniform, but now I feel like I do recognise him.

'You had the famous absconder that we kept bringing back.'

He's grown a beard since then, but I know exactly the child he is referring to from a few years ago. I feel a great relief. 'Yes, of course I remember you.' And an associated memory pops into my head and out of my mouth. 'You were here so much we bought in a stock of your favourite biscuits.'

We all laugh over that.

The bearded policeman returns to the matter at hand. 'Sky was very clear that you did not touch her. It's an odd one. We can only surmise she was *told* to say that. So, I'm sorry to say that perhaps there will be more to come.'

'Yes, I think so, too. You said earlier that Avril's story didn't add up.'

'No, it didn't. I asked her why she recorded the scene instead of going to help her sister. She said it was to prove that you were cruel. So I asked her to tell me more about this cruelty, which she couldn't. I asked her directly if you'd been cruel to her. She said no. And so I asked her if her mum had encouraged her to say and do these things.'

'And?'

'Well, she didn't answer. But that was enough of an answer, if you see what I mean.'

Maz comes back into the conversation with another one of her timely interventions. 'Look. The girls and you are getting along well. Much better, perhaps, than anyone could have anticipated a week ago. Of course Hanna will struggle to process the fact that the girls are happier and healthier. That's going to be a really tough thing for her to deal with. She won't want to hear the girls say nice things about you. You've told me that you've heard Sky on the phone to her mother at least twice.' Here she pauses deliberately. 'Do Claire and Charlie know about that, by the way? And has it been pointed out to them that it makes a complete joke of going to the bother of organising supervised contact?'

'Not yet, but they'll know about it in a minute.'

'Perhaps innocently, and no doubt with the best of intentions, Sky has been telling her mother about what a nice time she's been having while she's here,' Maz goes on. 'In my view, and knowing what I know about Hanna, she'll want to undermine that situation and do her best to regain control.'

The police radio cackles into life at that moment. Officer One says they have to leave straight away. 'But I'll make sure that the report is written up and reflects not only what we've seen here tonight, but also captures some of the thoughts about what might be going on beneath the surface.'

Lloyd shows them to the door. Claire and Charlie are yet to return, which leaves Maz and me alone in the kitchen.

'I'm just going to come straight out and say it. I don't think I want them here in the house any longer.'

'I completely understand,' Maz says. 'And you've coped brilliantly under really challenging circumstances. But think about it. If you hand in notice on this placement now, it will make you look guilty.'

Lloyd returns at that moment. 'We're not guilty of anything,' he says.

A pained expression passes over Maz's face. I know she is trying to help, but she is managing several things here. Perhaps she isn't being entirely straight with us. It doesn't help her much if we give notice. It creates more work. Other issues – such as funding and what her manager will say – are probably affecting her words as much as concern for our reputation.

'We'll just have to keep an eye on it,' she says, brightly.

I hate it when they say that.

Claire and Charlie come back in. Charlie looks pretty ineffective to me. He's in his thirties, and I've only just met him, but I'd say that he has an air to suggest that the whole episode this evening has been entirely distasteful to him. Perhaps social work is not his initial career of choice, or perhaps it has become that way and he has changed his mind about early convictions. Or perhaps he's just under the thumb of his boss. I'll find out. He hasn't said very much in front of Claire. She's far more dominant, cutting across him each time he opens his mouth. I don't like Claire at all.

And I think the dislike is mutual.

Sometimes being known as something of a public face in the fostering world, being the author of books about children in care and writing frankly about my own experiences of the same thing, can upset some people in the sector. If that's the case then those are her issues, but I'm here in my own home having to work out what to do and how to do it. I'm not going to get much help from their direction.

'I think you should go and talk to Avril,' Claire says, looking pointedly at me.

I'm fed up with people telling me what I 'should' do.

I don't feel like talking to Avril at all. I have to remind myself that actually, for all her talk and underhandedness, she's only a child. Her actions, unpleasant though they have been, are more likely to have been at her mother's instigation than her own. She is yet to be taught how to behave in a more sociable way, and that's not her fault. And Sky's so young. I'm sure she doesn't really understand quite what she's doing and the serious implications and repercussions that it might have had. And might still have, for all I know.

I feel another rush of anger. This time directed at Hanna. What is she doing getting her children to behave like this and do her dirty work? And what about their father? Where is he in all this? What a family dynamic I have inadvertently got myself caught up in. I don't share all my thoughts and these complicated feelings with Maz. After this evening's events I'm not in any mood to trust. I walk them all to the door, feeling somewhat dejected by Maz's final comments, as well as Claire's. Lloyd and I have been through a lot as foster carers over the years. We know that when things get tough it depends entirely on the individual social worker as to whether we are supported or thrown to the bears. The processes in fostering tend to be 'open for interpretation' – that's the diplomatic version, anyway.

I want to like Maz. I want her to be a decent, supportive social worker that we can develop a good working relationship with in the long term, but experience has taught us to be prepared in case it turns out that she is not. Right now the jury is out.

As I return to the warmth and light of the kitchen, brighter now that all the uninvited guests are finally gone from it, I hear Lloyd rounding up the children. It has been another late night for them, filled with bizarre sights and strange adults – but none of them seem fazed. There is even an excitement in the air, the sort that comes from the disruption to normal routine.

There's no sign of Avril, but Sky is there with the others, beaming away at me. There's something about her face that seems different, though. I wonder whether I detect a degree of concern.

Or perhaps remorse.

Chapter Twelve

Over the next few days the house calms down. Lloyd and I work hard to try and make sure that there is no further direct impact on the other children.

Sky becomes clingy. It's as if she needs to be with me all the time. This isn't unusual, but it's a stage in the attachment process that can be testing for a foster carer, and Sky has it in the extreme. She's like my little shadow around the house, even following me to the loo, waiting outside the door for when I come out again, and sometimes making me jump when I forget that she'll be there. After a little bit of practice she's become quite proficient at slicing off the top of her boiled egg with a knife. She can, after her feast, carefully leave behind what looks like a perfectly formed egg. Such a change from the first monstrous mashing of shell and white and yolk the first time she tried. I teach her to gently pack it with kitchen roll and turn it upside down in the egg cup to paint a face or pattern. We are beginning to curate quite an exhibition on the kitchen shelf.

But I also sense that she is worried about something. When I was in care myself I remember the feeling of being scared that something would happen if I said anything. My adoptive mother was an extremely mixed-up individual who could be terribly cruel towards me, partly because she was suffering so much herself. But the consequences of the psychological hold she had on me were awful. I sense something similar going on with these girls.

With a little encouragement from Lily we have been getting Sky on the trampoline every day, for at least a short while, even if it's cold outside. She enjoys it, I think. The shrieks and giggles suggest that she loves being on the trampoline, but of course it's the health benefits that I want to encourage, in addition to the fun. The Looked After Children's nurse has been to visit every week since Sky and Avril arrived. We are working hard to lose the weight from Sky and put it on to Avril, and today will mark her third visit.

Both girls complained about headaches and sore eyes at the first consultation, and these symptoms, along with what I noticed about Sky's wee and her initial reluctance to drink water, make me think that they might both be dehydrated. I try very hard to keep their hydration levels topped up. Sky is now easier in this regard. I let her choose her own drinking bottle which I keep topped up with water. She's loving owning it. Avril is more resistant. She keeps demanding fizzy drinks. I keep explaining how harmful they are. Whenever I do this I receive texts from Hanna informing me that Avril is entitled to make her own choices. I do not engage.

Today the nurse, Bridget, is happy with the way the girls' health is going. Sky has lost another two pounds, the same amount as last week – not that it is really easy to see. That's four pounds in total, and Bridget says she can already see a difference, which is pleasing. She congratulates me. While I can't actually see where the weight has come off, I do think that Sky is a little more mobile than she was. She's walking more happily – and now unaided – down the stairs, and no longer has to swing her legs out to help move her body up the stairs.

Buoyed by these successes, I decide to take Sky out for a walk and some extra exercise. As my little shadow, she is only too happy at the suggestion. We take the dogs to the park.

When we did this a day or two after she first arrived, she cried because even though it was only a short distance, it hurt her legs. She was so unfit, and still is – but I'm holding on to what the nurse has said and telling myself that we're making progress. Everything's going in the right direction, even if it isn't always easy to see. There is a slight camber on the road down to the park, so she enjoys the easy walk down – but still makes a huge fuss on the way back. She keeps stopping and crying and saying that she can't do it. I hold her hand and try to pull her up the tiny little hill. Even using the word 'hill' is an exaggeration, really. Two of my neighbours who are well into their eighties fly past us, stepping into the road to overtake. They look towards us with compassion as they overhear Sky's struggle.

Everyone in my area is lovely, and the fact that we foster is widely known; most make allowances for that and are supportive. Our immediate neighbours have all gone out of their way to welcome and be friendly to all the children, apart from one who lives a little way up the road. He voiced his opinion that the people coming forward as victims of Jimmy Savile years ago were 'making a fuss and should get over it.'

He seems to be the only one who really objects to our life choices. For some reason he doesn't seem to like what my family and I do. Once, when he walked past me while I was helping with respite for a child who had a little traumatic episode while out walking, the horrible man said, 'Surprise, surprise. Another naughty child. You need to keep it under control.'

Trauma can pop up anytime. It needs no invitation or triggers. It has nothing to do with being naughty; it's just there lurking in the background. But it wasn't worth explaining this to him. If I had half the chance, I think I would have given him a piece of my mind. But I didn't – not to spare his feelings, but because I didn't want to add to the child's distress. I think he knew I wouldn't retaliate, which is probably part of why he said it. People abuse others because they feel they can. (One day I'll have it out with him. One day!)

By the time we reach the top of the incline (and I'm using the word incline very generously), the dogs look bored. Sky seems to be struggling with more than just the climb, though.

'Sky? Is everything all right?'

She stops. 'Please don't get rid of me; I don't want to leave.'

'Oh, Sky! I don't want to get rid of you.'

'I didn't want to say those things I said. Hanna told me to.'

I put my hand on her shoulders so that she is looking at me directly. 'Thank you for telling me that, Sky. That's seriously brave and brilliant.'

I can't lie to her, though. 'Long term, I can't say if you stay or not. That's not my decision – it's up to the judge when your case goes back to court in a few months.'

I don't really know if these words mean anything at all to her. She's had so little life experience: I know that she has hardly been out anywhere or done anything. Even so, I get a strong sense that she carries an innate perception – and somehow understands.

She nods, with a weary wisdom that goes way beyond her years.

I reach out for her hand.

She pulls away sharply. 'Why do you keep trying to hold my hand?'

'Because we are just about to cross the road and, if I'm with a child, my instinct is to hold the child's hand – any child,' I laugh. 'When Lloyd and I are out together we both do it, without thinking – reach out for a child's hand. It's just something we are so used to. It's kind of instinctive.'

She still looks puzzled.

'But *why* do you hold a child's hand?'

'To keep you safe,' I say.

She stops again. 'Hanna never kept me safe.'

Chapter Thirteen

I know this sounds mad, but Sky's knickers remain a big mystery – and I find myself unduly preoccupied by it.

I simply have no idea what she is doing with them.

I keep buying packs of knickers and leaving them in Sky's room so that she has access to plenty. The packets get opened, and they gradually disappear. It's utterly bewildering.

Each day I pick her laundry up off the floor and search for dirty knickers. I ask her where they are. She just shrugs, and there are no answers.

Her weight loss continues slowly, but means that she can wear some more interesting clothes – even some that are a little more feminine and less shapeless. Because of the peculiar restrictions that are associated with the Section 20, I'm not able to take her for a haircut yet. This particular necessity does not come under the 'delegated authority' that I have (it would usually, but nothing about this placement is 'usual' and Hanna has specifically resisted it), so although she really needs a good trim, that can't happen yet. I've managed to tease out more knots, which make her look a little less odd. Her hair still smells, but much less than it did – although she never uses the shampoo unless I wash her hair at the sink with Lily and set up the 'salon' for them. In many ways, things are going well, or are at least improving.

I just wonder where those knickers *are*.

What could she possibly be doing with them?

I look in all the drawers. I look *behind* the chest of drawers. I think really hard about where the hiding places are in the room. I look underneath the bed and spot one of her teddies. I grab that as prized treasure – if she hasn't missed it for a few days, then I have a rare opportunity to wash it without her noticing. My search hasn't quite been in vain.

As I reach for the teddy, I sniff under the bed. The old Sky smell is here. I lie down on the floor and as I turn my head, I discover a whole little world. Looking up at the base of the bed, I see that she has drawn all over the wood. There are pictures of a figure – with sticks and weapons – hitting a smaller person. The same images repeat again and again. I guess the larger figure is Hanna and the other one must be Sky. Sky didn't appear to be bruised when she arrived – and we've seen plenty of that over the years. It seems very advanced for a six-year-old to be depicting a 'symbolic' beating, though.

I go and get my phone to take some pictures. Not only do I need to share them with Charlie and Claire, but I also want to study the images myself to try and understand more about what's going on for Sky. I don't really know what to make of them.

That smell, though. As I position myself flat on the floor again for a closer inspection, I finally realise where she has been putting her dirty knickers.

My first reaction is one of annoyance.

She has carefully cut an opening in the mattress. It's a smallish slit, one that would easily go unnoticed. I put my hand in and pull out dozens of pairs of knickers. Out they all come from the hole like a string of handkerchiefs from a magician's hat. Most of them just need a wash. The way that she has loaded them over time into this secret hold means that the oldest are the last to come out.

Here they are: the original sin. The first pair that she arrived with: the stinkers.

Oh God, I feel sick. The mattress has evidently held much of the smell in for the last month, but my goodness it's out now.

I look at the offending pants from arm's length. Crustations of wee and poo, and oh my God, the smell. I can't tell you quite how disgusting they are.

I drop them on the floor next to the others.

I go down to the kitchen to find a bag, because actually, I have a small dilemma on my hands here. My first instinct is to get them as far away from the house as possible. Is the amenity tip open today? But I have been read the riot act on the small print of a Section 20. We have to keep all items of clothing, wash them and give them back to the birth family.

A bit of me feels mischievous and wonders whether I ought to simply package them up and send them through the post to Hanna. It would make me feel good for about five minutes, but I know that it's a childish reaction. So I don't reach for an envelope. Instead I go and get a bag and go back upstairs to retrieve them.

To my horror, they have gone.

The dogs have escaped upstairs; someone, not me, has left their gate open.

I find my naughty dogs hiding in the garden. They are so small that they fit through the cat flap. Dotty has the knickers between her front paws and is licking them enthusiastically, while Douglas stands by wagging his tail, with a second pair trailing from his mouth. Dotty sees me coming and leaps up with them between her teeth. She isn't going to give up her spoils easily. A Keystone-Cops-style chase ensues, with me dashing between pots of geraniums and round flower beds to try and grab them back. If this were being filmed there would be a version of 'Yakety Sax', the Benny Hill theme, playing over the scene, perhaps with some canned laughter for good measure. I'm not sure that the dogs have ever had quite this much fun, and they pant and bark around the garden excitedly with their filthy treasures.

Eventually I get hold of them, but my victory involves a physical grapple with Dotty – which means I have touched the knickers with my bare hands. I throw them in the bag, wash my hands thoroughly – and make a point not to let either dog kiss me for the rest of the day.

I gather up all the remaining pants and sort them into piles – those that need to be burnt and those that can be washed and saved. I can dispose of the ones that I have bought her that can't be salvaged. We have a fire bin in the garden. It's much better than shredding and is good for small fires. I throw the stinky knickers into it, followed by a lit match, and watch them burn.

The dogs are still sniffing.

I phone the nurse (who is already aware of, and amused by, my knicker concerns) and tell her that I have finally found them.

Nurse Bridget has a strong Irish brogue and a great sense of humour. I've developed a good relationship with her over the last few weeks, and she roars with laughter when I explain about the dogs running off with the offending objects.

'Oh, stop it,' she says. 'My eyes are leaking,' and she bursts into another guffaw.

'It's okay now because I burnt them,' I say, which sets her off again.

After we stop laughing, I say, 'But seriously, you know, I still haven't seen her body properly. What if she has sores, or an infection of some sort?'

Bridget agrees that this is likely. 'Well, between us, perhaps young Sky will feel comfortable enough to tell us if she is itchy or sore.'

'I've seen her scratch her legs and arms at times, but whenever I ask if she is okay she stops.'

'I don't like the sound of that.'

Bridget arranges to come over the next day.

Chapter Fourteen

Avril remains an enigma. She still keeps herself to herself as much as she can. She speaks when spoken to and is outwardly polite. I can't help feeling that she has the capacity for mischief and disruption at any moment. She comes from a home environment where state institutions are to be distrusted, and as foster carers we represent one of those state institutions. We are, therefore, fair game. Authority figures are no doubt seen as adversaries, and it's a fine line to walk when I am busy trying to maintain some kind of order in my household.

And yet at times, perhaps when she feels insecure, she will come and just 'be' in my space, but won't say or do anything. She might come and sit in my studio when I'm working and be right in my face, but she doesn't ask for anything, and after a while she will just get up and disappear back to her room. She obviously wants to be there, because she shows up voluntarily, but at the same time she seems uncomfortable. Perhaps she has something on her mind. I can't tell if she is really reaching out or not. She's certainly too close for comfort at times, but I genuinely think she has a lack of judgement about acceptable spatial distancing. So far I have just smiled and let it be. I don't want to frighten her away. I wonder idly if she might have a boyfriend, or at least have designs on a boy. She's the right age for all of that to have begun, and she seems gradually to be taking more care of her appearance. She has made two separate, polite requests – one for a particular type of hair conditioner, and one for some razors. I am taking these as positive signs. I have also noticed that there is a little make-up on her bedside table. I wonder if she knows how to use it. I would like to help her, but I don't know where to begin without being patronising and intrusive.

Another little change is that Avril has started to go into town by herself. It's only a ten-minute walk away. I've given out a decent amount of pocket money over the weeks she has been with us, and when she is out I see the results: it goes on energy drinks and sweets. She keeps them in her drawer, and in the stinky suitcase. So it's a development of sorts, going out of the house, and I'm pleased that she's getting some fresh air, but it's not something that I'm particularly keen to encourage when it results in more poor food and drink choices. And we still see no sign of her building real relationships either at school or at home. The trips into town seem to be solitary.

Her conversations are awkward, but we all keep pressing on – and hope she feels more relaxed, and will continue to feel more relaxed, as time goes on.

School is not going terrifically well for either of the girls. The journey there in a taxi is at least an hour and a half each way, probably nearer two hours for the first leg in the morning traffic. This means the girls are constantly tired, more tired than they should be after an ordinary school day. It means that they have less free time than they should, and less fresh air. It makes play dates difficult to arrange because even if they do find friends, what other parent is going to want to drive all the way across the county so their child can get together with Avril or Sky for a few hours, when some other friend will be in walking distance of where they live? Not only is it hideous for such young people every day – it is also four hours of unsupervised contact. The taxi driver has told me that Avril is constantly on her phone, often to the same person. 'Hanna' is confirmed as a frequently heard name, but he also thinks she's talking to a boy. Perhaps the boyfriend thing isn't so far-fetched. And it's not the poor taxi driver's responsibility to monitor what's going on. All in all, it's not a satisfactory arrangement – but there is no other real option. Moving schools while they are on what may be a relatively short-term placement is not a practical answer. They are not children who need even more disruption to their educational careers. It's another intractable problem in the Rubik's cube of social care: one solution disturbs another. Foster carers don't magically live near the schools their foster children might attend. So we deal with the tiredness and the taxis.

We are to meet with Charlie, the girls' new social worker, again soon – although he has already cancelled two meetings, explaining that he has had some emergencies to deal with. I don't doubt that for a minute, but I do feel that these two are a slow emergency all on their own. I realise more every day that the years of emotional abuse and neglect that they have suffered must have been horrendous. I feel particularly for Avril, as she has been in this abusive setting for the longest: more than 14 years. Sky has been there for six and, though Sky clearly displays signs of being abused, I think that Avril is in deep. There are fewer opportunities to get in and support a child as they get older. Much of the support work has to come as a result of their own desire to feel better. And that's really difficult for these two: they have developed a culture and a way of thinking, a whole way of life in fact, that is so different from ours.

Lloyd keeps a regular check on Hanna's Facebook. She hasn't put anything new up. Maybe after the incident with the police she has backed off. That's a preferable conclusion to draw than the idea that she may simply be biding her time and plotting what to do next.

Bridget arrives with her portable scales and height chart. She gives me a wink as she comes in, and I nearly begin giggling again. She is a ray of sunshine and the perfect matronly character to be in the role of the Looked After Children's nurse. I don't doubt that in her time she has seen it all. Before I call the girls, I talk about my observations and concerns – and some of the small wins.

She smiles. 'It's also time to book a dental appointment.'

'Yes.' It sounds simple, but this can be tricky sometimes. It's all down to the communication between the child's social worker and the dentist, and Charlie is yet to do anything approaching effectual as far as I'm concerned.

Bridget says that she'll email and chase the social worker. 'I haven't met him yet, so it's about time we made our acquaintances anyway.'

We call the girls down; Avril first.

Avril walks into the kitchen and, to our amazement, has her hood down. In the whole time she has been here I have not seen her head, only fragments of her face under her curtain hair. She has been in my house for a month, but I'm not entirely sure I would be able to pick her out of a line-up. I look at her smile, and her beautiful features. I manage to avoid saying the words that want to burst out of my mouth: 'Oh Avril! It's so wonderful to see you. You're such a pretty girl.' I don't want to scare her. But I needn't have bothered with the restraint, because Bridget reacts anyway.

Avril illuminates.

The redness to her face has lifted a little, I think. Bridget weighs Avril and congratulates her for putting on three pounds. I think about her diet and suspect that the weight gain isn't simply down to my cooking, but to the bags of sweets and bottles of sugary energy drinks she is consuming. So, although it is certainly a step in the right direction, I know that there is plenty of work to be done on educating her about a healthier diet.

When Avril leaves to go back upstairs, Bridget walks over and closes the door behind her, so that she isn't overheard.

'That redness on her face,' she says, in quite a conspiratorial tone. 'I've seen it before on children. When I worked overseas.'

She pauses, and when I don't catch on immediately, she says, 'It's from dirty bedding, or whatever she sleeps on.'

'But I wash the children's bedding every week, on a high temperature cotton wash.'

'I don't doubt it. But if she's been living in squalor for years – and there are plenty of indications that she might have been – then she may easily have had skin infections that went untreated.'

'Skin infections?'

'Scabies, or bites from insects, or even infected eczema.'

Bridget asks me then if I have seen any signs of Avril having a period.

'No, nothing.' I've thought about this already. Avril is 14 and there is a chance she may just be a late starter, but it's also a possibility that through malnutrition and stress her body may actually be struggling to get there.

Bridget echoes my thoughts.

'Does she still seem stressed?'

'Yes, a little. I think so. But not by the move into care. I think because her parents – or at least her mum – is constantly phoning and messaging her.'

Bridget repeats almost exactly what Maz had said to me previously. 'I hate the phones. Don't you hate the phones? It's the very worst thing that could have happened to children coming into care.'

'The very people who have abused them still have access to them,' I agree.

'And there is no bloody law in place to prevent it!'

The famous Children Act, written in 1989, and updated in 2004 and 2017, remains out of date. It has no mention of technology and how this should be managed, so Bridget is absolutely right.

She goes on to say that she believes Avril is depressed. 'But I'm not a clinical psychologist, so that's only an opinion as a nurse.'

The social worker will need to ask his manager to have a physiologist make an assessment of Avril – and that could take months. My first impressions of Charlie haven't convinced me that he is particularly dynamic – I didn't get any sense of an urgency to get things done. I share a diplomatic version of my thoughts with Bridget.

'Hmmm. Well, my advice is to just keep getting as much good food into her as you can, along with plenty of water – and keep reinforcing the idea that she is a good person.'

'Yes, will do.'

'Oh, and off the record?'

I very much like a 'close the door' or 'off the record' moment, and give a nod of encouragement.

Bridget goes on. 'I have spoken to a colleague, another nurse who knows this family. She says that mum Hanna has displayed serious mental health concerns for years, but because she is bright enough to do her research, she knows exactly what entitlements she has. She's managed to keep interventions by the authorities and NHS out.'

'Well, that would fit exactly with my experience of her.'

'I know that social services have offered house clearances and cleaning, day care for the children, taxis to get the children to school, food deliveries. In fact, just about everything you can think of – but she has refused it all.'

Some people are too proud to accept help when it is offered, but this feels more like calculated resistance. I don't really understand.

'Do you know anything about the father? About John Wiseman?'

'Not much. He has multiple sclerosis and is confined to a wheelchair.'

'So Hanna's definitely driving all the decisions?'

For not knowing much, Bridget has plenty to say. 'I think he used to be quite vocal and has openly disagreed with Hanna, but seems to have lost his fight. We understand that he sleeps in the chair and never has a bath. Hanna won't let anyone in to help him either.'

'Why don't they force their way in?' I ask.

'Because the laws protect them. Privacy trumps safety here.' She pauses for a moment. 'In the same way that the lack of laws around children and mobile phones protect the paedophile.' She rolls her eyes. 'It's bloody ridiculous if you ask me.'

I'm inclined to agree with her. But it's Sky's turn next, and I call her in to be weighed and measured.

As usual, her face lights up into one big beaming smile as she enters the room.

'Wow, Sky, you look great,' Bridget exclaims.

It's another moral dilemma: getting the balance right between building self-esteem and being too image-conscious. Do we risk contributing to the image-related issues the girls might have by focusing on size and weight and 'improvement'? Or do we risk further neglect and health issues if we don't help with self-esteem? I watch Sky's face light up with the compliment, and it's enough to convince me that we are doing the right thing. We need to keep working on self-esteem, but we need to make sure that we are doing it in a healthy way.

She stands on the scales. Even I notice that her eyes are appearing out of her cheeks. A month ago they seemed so sunken into the excess flesh that it was difficult to see them at all. There is definite improvement.

Sky has lost two pounds.

'Congratulations, Sky!'

'Really well done,' I congratulate her too. 'All that wonderful effort of bouncing on the trampoline and playing in the garden and going for walks is paying off.'

She hasn't got taller yet, though with a new shape developing and a slimmer profile, she gives the illusion of looking 'longer' and the suggestion that she is growing.

'Oh, well done you. Good work. I'm sure Louise will let you have a treat for being so fantastic,' Bridget says.

I get this. We need to show the girls that life is all about balance: it's OK to have a biscuit or two if you run about and get exercise.

I notice Sky itch her arm once more, as does the nurse.

'Can I look at your arm please, Sky?' Bridget asks.

Sky offers up her arm – something she hasn't done before. Such a small thing, but I'm really pleased. It's another sign to me that she is relaxing more and more.

The nurse gently rolls up Sky's sleeve. I confess that I am fascinated. I have not seen anything of Sky's body other than her head and hands. She keeps everything well hidden, shrouded in clothing, and will not let me even go into the bathroom with her; nor am I allowed in her room when she dresses.

The nurse looks at the lesion shaped as a red circle. We both know what that is: ringworm. A fungal infection of the skin, though one that's caused by a fungus, not a worm, in spite of the name.

'Can I look at the other arm, too?' Bridget asks gently.

There is further evidence of ringworm there, too.

'I expect that's a little bit itchy, isn't it? I can give you some special cream to help that.'

Sky shrugs.

'And legs? Can we see those?'

'No.' Sky gives a determined shake of the head to accompany the flat verbal refusal.

'That's okay,' Bridget says. 'You've done brilliantly today. Off you go then, Sky; time to play again. I'll see you next week.'

Sky heads off once more, giving the trademark beam as she disappears through the door.

'I'll get a prescription sorted out for some topical antifungals.'

'Thank you. The trouble will be getting Hanna's permission to administer them. As we know, she's against any intervention, even if it helps.'

'We haven't seen Avril's arms, but I'll guess that both girls have the same condition. You do have your work cut out for you with this pair, don't you?'

143

'I certainly do.'

'I suggest more bathing and clean clothes every day.'

'I'll change their bedding every day too, if that will help.'

And I'll talk to the doctor to see if there is any way round needing Hanna's permission for the antibiotics. I'll get the doctor to liaise with the social worker directly – whether that will make any difference or not, I don't know.'

'What about the other children?' I ask. 'Are they at risk?'

'Good question. Fortunately it's still winter, so they are all wrapped up most of the time.'

'And neither Sky nor Avril are hugging anyone.'

'No,' Bridget laughs. 'But couldn't they both just do with a big hug, so?'

'Absolutely.'

'To get back to your question: given the covering up for the cold and the dearth of cuddles, I doubt there are any infections – but both cats and dogs can catch ringworm, and then pass it on to the humans who touch them. So keep an eye on it all, mind.'

'Yes, will do.'

'And don't be sharing any towels!'

Chapter Fifteen

It's just before Christmas, the week after school has finished. I've sat through endless carol concerts, and the Nativity plays are over. I book online tickets for both Lily and Sky to see *Frozen II*. I offer it to the boys and to Avril, but unsurprisingly they decline. I am delighted to get the 4pm slot. It will be dark and a bit Christmas-magical with twinkling lights everywhere. I have already been to the supermarket to buy sweets. I'll buy them a drink inside the theatre, but honestly the prices of snacks and treats are crazy, especially when multiple children are involved. I'm also mindful that it is important that they know that big treats every time they go out aren't a given. It's unrealistic, especially on a fostering allowance that still thinks we are in the 1970s and is yet to fully account for decimalisation, let alone inflation.

Sky is beyond excited. She has been fizzing up over the final days of term, overwhelmed by the Christmas activity anyway, and she has never been to the cinema before. Of itself this isn't unusual – a number of children that we have fostered over the years have experienced their first cinema trip with us.

People are horrified when I tell them this, but I hadn't actually been to the cinema myself until Tim, my first boyfriend, took me to the Moulin Rouge cinema in Headington, Oxford, when I was in my mid-teens. It was an art cinema where they showed old black-and-white films and a lady played the piano live for ambience. Oh, forgive me for romanticising, but what a fabulous date for a 17-year-old boy to take an impressionable young girl on. And what a fabulous first movie experience memory to retain. Even reliving it now, that memory has a certain silver-screen quality to it, and I float around in a vaguely Vivien-Leigh-esque way.

Sky is full of questions. 'How big is the screen?'

'Bigger than our house!' I say.

She lights up. 'How loud will it be?'

'Very. But that's what makes it exciting. Sometimes it's so loud that you can feel some of the sounds inside you like a vibration.'

She is beside herself as we leave the house.

'Bye, Lloyd. Bye, Vincent. Bye, Jackson,' she calls out. 'We're going to the big, loud cinema!'

'Enjoy,' Lloyd says, absent-mindedly. No one is really paying any attention to us. Lloyd is watching *Star Wars* with Vincent, and Jackson is gaming. Avril is upstairs in her room, no doubt communicating with her mother.

We park the car, and as I reverse I can see Sky's face in the mirror. Lily is in the passenger seat next to me and follows my gaze. She smiles, enjoying Sky's enjoyment, just as I am. She really is turning into a wonderful young woman.

We lock the doors and walk across the car park, with me constantly saying 'look out' or 'be careful' as cars come and go in the early darkness of a winter night. We walk to the entrance and – wow – her face is a picture as she looks at the big posters of all the films locked inside glass frames. Through the entrance doors she stops still and looks upwards, staring transfixed at the high ceiling and all the flashing lights and action. Next her eyes catch sight of something even more exciting: sweets everywhere!

We line up for a drink and, melted by Sky's astonishment about the whole experience, I cave in against my better judgement and buy the children's snack tray of a drink plus three items of their choice. I have extra sweets secreted in my bag. This is going to be such a lovely event.

I buy myself a Diet Coke which, like everything else in this place, is outsize, and we carry our spoils forward through the ticket control. An usher directs us towards our screen, and Sky is practically dancing with delight. She has evidently never experienced anything like it. If even I'm shocked by the size that the fizzy drinks are dispensed in, then the scale of everything must seem unreal to Sky.

'Okay, do we need the loo before we go in? I'm going, so you'd better just come with me anyway.' I know that Sky wouldn't ask of her own accord.

Next it's time to find our seats. Lily patiently shows Sky how the number on the ticket corresponds to a particular spot. Sky grasps it quickly and beams like a *Mastermind* winner when she locates G1, G2 and G3 for us.

We munch on our excessive snacks while the auditorium is still partially lit through the advertisements. Sky is in heaven. She keeps looking at me with that perfect round 'o' of a mouth in her round head, as if she is auditioning for the face of the 'wonder and amazement' emoji. I shed a quiet little tear for no reason at all, other than enjoyment of the joy I am watching on her shining face.

Lily shares a knowing smile with me. She had never been to the cinema either when she first came to us. She will know exactly what Sky is feeling.

I don't think I see much of the film itself. I'm too busy watching Sky and Lily as they smile and cry their way through *Frozen II*. This sideshow is more entertaining to me than the film.

It sets me off thinking about all that we have and don't fully appreciate. Maybe we all have too much. So much that it becomes impossible to really take pleasure in some things. Great pleasures come to us so quickly and easily that they can just as quickly and easily be taken for granted. Like me, I think Lily is enjoying the experience more because she is reliving it through Sky's eyes, activating prior memories to see it all afresh once more.

When I left art school, I was an artist-in-residence at a well-known private school which at the time seemed to be populated mainly by the offspring of media types. Part of my brief was to help start the new autumn term with a carnival. I did lots of research into what that might look like in practice. I'd been to the Isle of Wight carnival, which I had really enjoyed, and of course Notting Hill carnival for the visual spectacle and costume and music ideas. On my first day I explained our project, bursting with enthusiasm and excitement. A willowy young teenager, whose perfect skin and long, blonde, perfectly tousled hair were built for modelling – and whose celebrity parentage I might easily guess at – looked pointedly away from me as I outlined my plans.

'I don't want to do it,' she said. 'I've just come back from Rio de Janeiro and an actual, proper carnival. This is pathetic.' I felt so deflated and silly for trying.

But watching these two beautiful girls, who have had so little, really, relative to some of their peers, and seeing them light up and feel wonderful in the cinema, makes me wonder who is richer. How disappointing life must have been for that model-in-the-making. How little joy she must have found in day-to-day living. It wasn't me that was inadequate for the job of creating a carnival. It's a cliché, but I realise in that moment of observation that 'inadequate' is not seeing and appreciating the joy of small things.

When we get back home, none of us want the magic to end. Sky and Lily get their 'special' blankets and snuggle up to re-watch the first *Frozen* film. All the children have at least one fluffy blanket. It's become a bit of a thing that has carried on over the years. Generally they are selected by favourite colour. Nothing fancy, not cashmere, just something soft from the Poundstretcher or the market. They last for years. They aren't just for snuggling up with, either. They all wear them as capes. And because they tend to be on the large side, they don't look like superheroes – they look like Vikings, who are not so much superheroes as conquerors. There are moments when they waft around in them like a little tribe. Sometimes I even let them wear them at the table when it's a blanket day. I don't actively encourage it, but it's just a bit of fun.

I make sandwiches, pour crisps into a bowl, but stop short of further fizzy drinks and make sure they both have big glasses of water. I am always reminding my foster children to drink water. I think that a lot of what professionals describe as challenging behaviour is actually rooted in poor mood caused by dehydration.

The boys come down to see how we got on, and pick up the vibe – or perhaps survival instincts kick in and they want food. Either way, they both shoot back up the stairs to bring down their blankets. Cushions and beanbags are arranged just so, and the soft Viking 'armour' adds to the *hygge* mix. As plates empty, I make further trays of sandwiches, and bring in yet more sweets for my little band of warriors – at peace for now.

Chapter Sixteen

I feel as though I've had a nice bonding time with Sky, but I've been brooding on Avril's strange 'wanting to be near me, but not engaging with me' behaviour. I am the adult, and it's time I reached out to her more fully. Without close girlfriends she will have no one to experiment with hair and make-up looks, and I sincerely doubt that Hanna is into that sort of thing either. In fact, I don't get the impression that Hanna is into any traditionally 'feminine' activities at all. I'm keen to show Avril how to apply the make-up she has, and to let her know that these harmless activities bring joy and confidence to our lives. We don't have to look like men to retain feminist credentials. In fact, in my view, women are more powerful the *less* like men we are. Anyway, Ru Paul et al. have no problem expressing their feminine side. Without wanting to enter a debate on gender and sexuality, I'm a firm believer that it is simply society that hard-wires us to focus on male or female pursuits. That's why I am so excited about the LGBTQI community. It gives us the opportunity to dismantle these old notions – though I am aware that, as with all groups, there are those who are more fanatical than others. People are people, after all.

I leave it for a few days, and then suggest that Avril and I could go shopping at the weekend. Just the two of us. At first she isn't thrilled by the idea.

'I thought we could get lunch in town, and you could

do with a few more clothes,' I add into the mix. 'It's probably easier to browse more grown-up shops without Sky. And I wouldn't mind a scoot round the big Boots store for some make-up for myself. You could have a look too, if you like.' The Boots still has good old-fashioned make-up counters that make the whole experience more fun and less clinical. I even manage to convince myself that it will all be terrific fun.

When Saturday arrives, Lloyd, in on the plan, has already lined up some DIY jobs that will involve the children. Not to mention letting them have a later start after the busy school week.

Avril and I are up early.

We drive into town and I ask her how it's going at school. She looks a bit awkward. 'Fine,' she says, in that meaningless way teenagers do.

I lead the conversation more directly. I ask about her friends and get a similar response.

'But is there anyone you would like to invite over to the house?' I persist. 'I'd be happy to drive and collect and return.'

She looks surprised by my offer.

'Oh, well. I thought that – I mean, Hanna—' She seems to check herself and stops whatever she was about to say, casting me a sideways look that I clock. We make awkward eye contact. I've learnt that car time with a teenager can be priceless in terms of gleaning knowledge about their thoughts or worries. I wonder what it was she thought, and what Hanna had to do with it. I wonder if Hanna has portrayed me as an old bag who couldn't be expected to do anything for Avril. It's not true at all, of course, but living in a house where the birth parent also seems to have a presence is an interesting experience.

We park and get out of the car, and I notice how awkwardly Avril's long limbs seem to be struggling under the weight of her oversized hoodie. She is, as ever, top to toe in black.

She suddenly says, without looking at me, 'Perhaps Josh could come over.'

'Is he your boyfriend?'

She shrugs, which I take as code for 'yes'.

For the girl who seems to have no real friends and be such a loner generally, I am thrilled. This is good news. But no sooner have I had that thought than concern creeps in to replace it. I doubt very much whether Hanna has had 'those' conversations with Avril. I'm also pretty sure that Avril will have missed the sex education sessions in Year 6 and beyond. I wonder if, like so many young people, she has got her ideas and knowledge about sex from porn sites. It's a phenomenon which explains why so many of my stepdaughters' friends – in their twenties – have decided to abstain from sex. It's a reaction to being strangled, slapped, spat at and peed on. It is the reality for many young women, and I can see why they are sick to death of it. I need to think of a way for Avril to learn about sex and love, and for that to happen fast.

First off, we scoot round a couple of fashion shops. Avril sees a pair of dungarees she likes. I smile to myself and think, *They are pretty dowdy and hard to get into.* 'Good choice. You can have them!' I say, quickly. And then I'm a little bit cross with myself. What am I thinking? I was at this stage once, and I have memories of wanting to show off my flesh, a body that I was proud of. Why not? After all, it's at its best when one is young. So many things flash through my mind – safeguarding and predators. It's a minefield. Why shouldn't young women wear what the hell they want? It's the predatory men that need to change.

In the same shop Avril tries on a fitted dress. She comes out of the changing room to show me, rather coyly, and she really does look amazing. I had no idea that she had any kind of figure. I haven't seen it before, hidden beneath all that shapeless clothing. I never want to elevate appearance above far more important aspects of character, but I do want to help her confidence, and I remember how awkward it feels as a teenager during puberty. 'Wow, Avril. You look great,' I tell her.

We actually have a very nice morning. While I couldn't go as far as to say that Avril is opening up, there is far less of the sullenness and front that she sports at home. I can see a vulnerability beneath the hard veneer she cultivates. She is into the 'punk/emo' look. As an ex-'punk/indie' aficionado myself (don't we all just love a label?), I am slightly baffled by the fact that it's still a thing. I recognise some of this clothing from my own teenage years. Avril wants fishnet tights to wear under her new black shorts. I go for those, too.

As we walk round the square at the centre of town, I lose Avril briefly. When I turn round and find her staring at the Ann Summers window display, I distract her by pointing out a sale sign for a less overtly sexual retailer, and hope that she has no idea about what she has just been looking at.

It does get me thinking, though. What stage has her relationship with 'Josh' got to? Is it something I need to be worried about yet? I didn't think so, but now, having seen her all dressed up and looking much older, I'm not so sure. On the way home I try to gauge a little more about him and how well they know each other. I ask about his family and where he lives and what he's like and what he wants to do – you know, the full list.

'Well, let's get him round. I'll even work out the buses.'

I'm already thinking that if he is a steady boyfriend, he will want to visit Avril quite a lot – and given the distances involved, 'Louise's taxi' idea is now off the table. Today has shown me a more grown-up Avril; I have caught a glimpse of the person she might become, beyond the sullen teenager who exists only to do her mother's bidding and thrives on causing upset. It is only a glimpse, though. When she gets back home, she runs upstairs and I hear the murmured tones of one side of a phone call. I hope it's Josh, but the nature of the conversation tells me otherwise.

'You're right. I'll do that,' she says.

And I know it's Hanna. When I call Avril down for dinner later the hoodie is back on, the shutters are down, and it is as if our morning together never happened.

Chapter Seventeen

The following Saturday Josh comes over.

I open the door to teeth. A lovely smile on a skinny, awkward young man. Like Avril, he is dressed head to toe in black, and also like her, he gives me the feeling of not quite fully inhabiting his own skin yet, not knowing where to put himself. He stands awkwardly in the hallway while I call Avril down. Her awkwardness matches his. Making her way down the stairs, her movements suggest that she doesn't have complete control of her limbs. Usually so light and soundless, she seems to thump down, sinking into each step. It's quite sweet to see all this nervousness.

'Hi,' she says, shyly.

'Aren't you going to invite Josh in?' I say, after several seconds of what feels to me like too much pause. I have already briefed Avril that the door rule remains important: if Josh goes up to her room then the door must be open. They escape upstairs. Soon I hear lots of giggling, something I have not heard from Avril before. I try and keep Sky away from her sister, which is tricky. Sky is desperate to make an impression with Josh, too. Sometimes foster children don't understand the social nuances of friends coming round. Vincent has complained a couple of times about Sky trying to take over his friends when they visit. I decide to take Sky out to the local animal sanctuary, where she can 'oooh' and 'awww' over fluffy and furry creatures, and leave her sister in peace for an hour or two. I forget that I will spend the outing fighting off Sky's requests to adopt everything she sees.

When we are home and it's time for Josh to go, I walk through the hall and past Avril's door (which has been left obligingly open as I requested), to see that Avril and Josh are engaged in a big snog. They've got over some of that shyness, then. I think to myself that we'd better have 'that' conversation about contraception. We definitely don't want any babies here at the moment, thank you. I also think about the wording of the email I am going to need to write to Charlie, their social worker. Tricky, and a little delicate, given that we haven't even met properly yet.

Meanwhile, I make up reasons to keep taking Avril out on drives in order to find time alone to talk to her. The car is a good place because we don't have to look at each other directly. I try to explain about consent, pressure, good sex and rubbish sex. I even explain that orgasms are good and that it is the aim of the partner to give her a nice one. I try to be as forthright as I possibly can. In my head, I keep hearing the conversation I had recently with my step-daughter and one of the young hairdressers about 'dry sex' and strangulation, though I don't bring this up with Avril, of course. I am so sad and scared for young women who think this is the only sexual activity available. I'm conscious also that the reporting of sexual violence in school is on the increase, and while Avril gives the appearance of being well able to take care of herself, I know that deep down she is very vulnerable. Girls, and some boys, are not safe in school – and this I find totally unacceptable. I blame the increased access to porn via the internet, which has presented a completely unhealthy and unrealistic representation of sex. My step-daughter told me that young women are rebelling against this kind of representation and growing their pubic hair, rather than having it all removed to look like a blow-up doll. I am so anxious to educate Avril, but I'm not sure she's quite ready for the Bring Back the Bush campaign. In spite of my upfrontness, I feel a little confused myself.

It takes Charlie several days to come back to me, but eventually I receive his reply. It includes this phrase:

I agree that under the circumstances you have described that it is likely that Avril may begin to have sexual relations with her boyfriend.

Well, I'm pleased that he's woken up to that possibility at least. I chat it through with Lloyd who, like me, thinks that the sooner Avril is on a form of contraception, the better.

But Avril is already ahead of me. Of course she is. She wants to go on the pill. Because Avril is on a Section 20, Hanna will need to give her consent. There is another delay as paperwork goes backwards and forwards once more.

Charlie reports back that Hanna flatly refuses for Avril to take any form of contraception. I'm not surprised. Her modus operandi simply seems to be to block and be objectionable. This protest, like the others, is about her – and not about Avril. I become angry, momentarily, and have to remember that negative energy is just not allowed in my house. I stole that from the mother of one of Lily's friends. We were discussing a bullying incident that had taken place amongst a few of Lily's friends. As usual with cases of bullying, there is an underlying cause that is sometimes rooted within the family itself. She was standing in my hallway collecting her child, and her words were unforgettable. She said, 'I'm not having this negativity in my house.' Her proclamation was accompanied by fantastically theatrical hand gestures. I thought it was a wonderfully clear-cut attitude that could fit a lot of things: just don't let it cross the threshold into the home. Choose to leave it at the front door.

I'm trying so hard to live by this mantra, but the negativity trickles into our house via Hanna on the phone. Some days I want to drown that phone in the washing-up bowl or run over it in my car. But I can't even take it away, because it's the property of Hanna.

I end up having a few careful conversations with Avril. They are careful because I know that she still talks to her mum daily. But on this subject, for once I sense rebellion in Avril.

'I'm not engaging in the no-contraception conversation with her,' Avril claims. 'It's my body, not hers.'

She's got a point. I decide to give the nurse a ring and see what sense she can come up with. Charlie is dithering, and I suspect scared of Hanna. Bridget informs me about something called 'Gillick competence.' I've never heard of it.

'Avril may have the right to choose herself without her mother's consent. Gillick competence allows young people under the age of 16 to make their own choices about medical issues such as contraception, or immunisation, for example, as long as they're properly informed.'

'I am all ears.'

'Have a chat with the doctor. I think it would be possible for Avril to go to the surgery and give consent to receive the pill for herself.'

Lloyd does some quick googling. 'Providing a child can demonstrate sufficient maturity and intelligence to understand the nature and implications of the proposed treatment, including the risks and alternative courses of actions,' he says, reading from his phone.

'Well, well.'

No point in waiting on it, so later that evening I knock on Avril's door.

'Can we have a chat about something?' I ask her.

She shrugs, but doesn't say no.

'Before we do, might you put your phone on the window-sill and turn it off?'

I can't have Hanna listening in to this – it will simply defeat the whole object. I don't expect Avril to do it, but to my surprise, she slides off the bed and makes a show of turning the phone off.

'There.'

I thank her. Then ask how she feels about getting going with a programme of contraception. I remind her about the reasons why this might be a good idea, starting with her age.

'I know all this. You're not telling me anything that I don't already know. I'm just annoyed with Hanna for not sorting it out,' she says, eventually.

'Well, what it comes down to is that in fact it's not Hanna's decision to make. It's yours.'

There is a pause.

'Really?'

'Really.'

I tell her about Gillick competence.

'That's all well and good, but—' she swallows. 'You know how Hanna has some strong views about education and social welfare?'

I certainly do. I've been on the receiving end of them. I nod.

'Well, she also has them about medication and the NHS.'

'Do you want to tell me about them?'

'Hanna and John are anti-everything to do with medicines – well, the stuff that's for profit. They fight big

159

companies. They've been working on a campaign to expose stuff about the whole thing, the whole—' She searches for the right words. 'You know. The big businesses who make and sell drugs and medical things.'

'The pharmaceutical industry?'

'Yes, them.'

This is the closest we have come to any kind of criticism of Hanna and John's lifestyle choices.

'That's a pretty big industry to take on by themselves.'

'Yup.'

'Do you think that your parents can win? Can they make the changes that they want to see on their own?'

She shakes her head.

I go back to the original question. 'Do *you* want to go on the contraceptive pill?'

Avril looks towards the window. I follow her eyes to see if she looks at the phone. She doesn't.

'Yes. Yes, I think I do. I mean…' She trails off and goes quiet and chews on her lip again.

I wait for a moment to see if she will finish. I think this conversation has been really hard for her. It is an enormous step forward in our relationship for her to feel that she can confide some of these feelings – while being critical of her parents. I don't push her.

'OK. So would you like me to sort out an appointment for you?'

She nods. 'Thank you.'

'Are you going to tell Hanna?'

'Yes. I think so. Yes, I think I am.'

She sounds as though she is convincing herself as well as me. I close the door quietly and leave her to her thoughts.

As soon as the lines are open the next morning, I call the surgery to book it. I know all the reception staff quite well these days – we've had many children who have come into our home and require a temporary registration while we hunt for paperwork, so they are used to my requests. They can fit Avril in in a week's time, and make it a double appointment so that there will be more time to talk everything through properly.

I email Charlie, Bridget and Maz, and inform them all that Avril would indeed like to give her own consent to go on the pill.

They all email back to say that this is good news. Bridget gives me a 'that was quick work!' winky face.

Chapter Eighteen

Finally we meet Charlie properly.

He arrives on time, carrying a big briefcase full of paperwork and a separate laptop bag. He takes some time setting up his mobile office in our kitchen. Dotty takes exception to him for some reason, so I put her in her little cage in the sitting room and shut the door. Her protests can be clearly heard, but there is nothing to do except ignore them. Lloyd raises an eyebrow as Charlie faffs around getting himself plugged in and organised.

'So, how are we all since the incident?' he opens, once he is finally settled.

He doesn't actually put inverted commas round 'the incident' as he says the words; nevertheless I can hear them.

'Okay, thanks,' I say, in a rather perfunctory way.

Lloyd nods politely.

'Good. Well, I thought I'd let you know that the police are no longer concerned after Sky made it clear to them that you didn't hurt her and, when we spoke to her that evening, she did admit that Hanna had told her to do it.'

I say nothing, but remember the way that Claire, his manager, had seemed to imply that there were other, as yet unspecified, complaints about me.

'Now, the important news is that another court date has now been arranged, this time to determine whether the girls will stay in care or go back home.'

'Do you think that they will go back home?'

His assured manner starts to fall away. 'Umm, no. Not really. But we never really know what will happen until the judge decides.'

We write the date in our diaries. It's in nearly two months' time, which in some ways feels an age away. We talk for a while about how the girls are doing more generally. He sits at the table with his laptop and writes it all down. If nothing else, he is meticulous in his record-keeping.

I explain that I need to make a dental appointment, but that he needs to be the one to sanction this.

'It needs to come from you in case Hanna says no. But it's really important. From what I can tell, I think Avril's teeth are in very poor order. I've encouraged her as much as I possibly can, but I don't think she cleans her teeth.'

He raises an eyebrow.

'It's much easier with Sky, given her age,' I explain. 'I stay with Sky each evening to watch her clean her teeth. We have the tooth timer and we have bought her a whizzy toothbrush that sings whilst she cleans, so she really likes that.'

Charlie writes more things down while I continue.

'But I can't seem to get Avril to take much of an interest in her health at all. She *is* gaining weight slowly – certainly not as fast as her sister is losing it. But there is a little progress in that department.'

'Well, that's good.'

'And she has on occasion worn her hoodie with the hood down – but nothing else until last weekend.' I explain about Josh and the sudden change in attitude towards clothing. 'Up until the weekend's expedition we had been buying clothes online, but they are all identical copies. She pretty much only wears a black hoodie and black jeans. She sometimes wears a white T-shirt underneath, but I only see it to wash it because she never takes the hoodie off.'

'Well, I think it's probably good. I don't know that I'm qualified to have an opinion on teenage fashion choices,' Charlie says.

I wonder what exactly he *is* qualified to have an opinion on, but keep that train of thought to myself. Reference to Josh brings us round naturally to the contraception issue. 'She's not actually on the pill yet. We had to make a second appointment.' I make it clear that Avril attended the first appointment by herself, since I didn't want to interfere with the Gillick competence process and be putting any kind of inadvertent pressure on Avril one way or the other. 'The doctor actually suggested a birth control implant,' I explain, 'rather than the pill for Avril. I think because it removes the danger of forgetting to take the pill every day, and I'm inclined to agree.'

Charlie looks a bit blank. I don't think female contraception is one of his areas of expertise.

'The implant is a plastic rod, about the size of a match. It goes under the skin on your upper arm. It's a very straightforward procedure. It doesn't hurt. You can have it removed at any time and it lasts for three years. We're booked in for next week. And I've said no to Josh coming round this weekend in the meantime!'

'Good, well, er, well done on all that,' Charlie says, keen to move on. We talk next about Sky's progress and how she is still struggling with school.

'But it's not just school itself: the long taxi journey isn't helping. And we know that it means that both girls are having unsupervised phone contact for four hours a day, five days a week.'

'Right.'

'And isn't it funny how Hanna hasn't felt the need to push hard for actual contact? I mean, we might have expected that by now,' I say.

'Yes, but contact is something that would require her to leave her house, and she evidently doesn't do that.' Lloyd articulates our conclusions from conversations we have had repeatedly in recent days.

'I see.'

Perhaps I'm changing my mind about Charlie. We seem to get on. I wonder if he is just overworked. And to be fair, I've never met an underworked social worker. I also suspect he doesn't have much leeway in decisions. Judging by what I've seen of bossy Claire so far, I think he's probably being told what to do and say by her. We agree another time and date in a few weeks.

'Meanwhile, call me if you need anything,' he says, busying himself packing up papers that have spread across the kitchen table. I can't work out why he needs the laptop and all the paper, but he presumably knows what he's doing.

To my surprise, I receive an email the following morning from Charlie. It is cc'd to Maz and the nurse, and confirms that he has sanctioned a dental appointment for the girls, since there is no record of them ever seeing a dentist. From what I have seen of their lack of commitment to oral hygiene, and from talking to the girls, I think he is probably right. So I get straight on to arranging the dental appointment. It isn't as straightforward as it was to get Avril in at the doctor's surgery. There's a long waiting list for an after-school appointment, but I'm offered a mid-morning slot in the week, in just a few days' time. I decide that the urgency of their need outweighs missing school, and it seems prudent to strike while the iron is hot.

Because of their long commutes, though, the timing of the dental appointment requires the girls to take the whole morning off school. Lloyd and I decide that by the time the taxi gets them to school after the appointment it would be time to come home again anyway – so we let the girls have the entire day off. They are excited, while our other children are singularly unimpressed.

'It isn't fair. I want a day off if they're having one,' Lily tries, sullenly.

I ignore the protests and claims of injustice.

On the day of the dental appointments I make sure that Sky has cleaned her teeth. I also notice that the daily dirty knickers are thrown on the floor along with her other clothes. I don't say anything, but clock this up as another small victory, before having a word with myself for silently 'cheering' dirty knickers. What has my world come to?

We sit in the dentist's waiting room. Charlie was right. Neither has been before so there is, understandably, some anxiety about what is about to happen. They keep asking questions, and there is fidgeting while we wait.

'Is it like a hospital?'

'Will it hurt?'

'Can we go in together?'

'Will I get fillings?'

'Will they drill my teeth?'

'Will I have to sit in one of those chairs?'

We're called in. I have made sure that the dentist knows that the girls are in care and that they haven't been to a dentist before – at all. I hope he will be gentle.

Sky is first. She sits down and beams as usual. She loves putting the protective glasses on and enjoys the sound of the dentist's chair manoeuvring into position. Her grin widens further.

'Open wide.'

The dentist looks in her mouth, and I can tell by the face he pulls that it's not good news. He calls out the teeth to his assistant. 'Upper doo-da eleventy-four, lower wot-not alpha foxtrot.' Even though it is a foreign language, a code that I can't decipher, the tone tells me there are issues. When he is finished, the dental nurse lets Sky choose a sticker. She is thrilled. While she is busy choosing between Peppa Pig and Spider-man he explains, in front of the girls.

'I'm shocked, if I'm honest. Fortunately these are her first teeth and will come out, so new ones will grow, but the back teeth are so rotten they are almost through to the nerve. If they don't come out soon Sky will be in a lot of pain.'

He goes on to tell me that it may require an operation at the hospital.

Sky stops rummaging in the sticker box and just sits down on one of the additional chairs staring at nothing. I wonder how she is processing all this. I give her what I hope is a reassuring pat on the shoulder. For the first time, she doesn't pull away.

Next in the chair is Avril. She was more nervous than her younger sister anyway, but that news seems to have increased her anxiety further. She has her hoodie right up and pulled out over her forehead – she is in hiding. Thankfully, the dentist is patient with her, as is the nurse.

When he has finished with Avril, I notice tears in his eyes. He turns away to compose himself. I'm surprised, as an experienced professional, that he's so affected. Until he speaks.

Turning back towards me, he hangs his head, but doesn't soften his words. He isn't being unkind, just truthful. He doesn't sugar-coat the prognosis. Well, he wouldn't, would he?

'All her teeth are damaged. There is irreversible decay in every tooth. For now we can give both girls fluoride treatments, and I can show them how to clean their teeth. We'll arrange for them to see the hygienist, who can offer guidance and advice. But I'm afraid Avril's teeth will need replacing by the time she is 18.'

He looks so sad, defeated by what he has seen in their mouths.

Avril double-checks. 'I have to have false teeth?'

He nods.

She starts to cry.

It's the first time I have seen a genuine emotional reaction since she arrived, and my heart goes out to her. Until now there have been smirks and smugness, sullenness and false politeness.

'These days children eat so many sweets, drink sugary squashes and fizzy drinks constantly. It's rotting their teeth and, sadly, Avril and Sky have not been cleaning their teeth. All that damage has been allowed to happen with nothing to stop it.'

We leave the dentist's surgery downcast. The girls are quiet, the atmosphere subdued.

When we get in the car Avril swallows and says, 'So. When is that appointment for the implant?'

Chapter Nineteen

For a couple of days, the household carries on nicely. Gradually the children seem to relax and get on more easily. Avril has been gaming with Jackson and the hood is down most of the time. Not only is that less intimidating for all of us, but I now feel that I would at least be able to pick her out from a line-up. She hasn't been wearing her new clothes, but then she hasn't seen Josh outside of school, and I get the impression that they are being saved for him.

Both girls' skin is starting to look a little better. The redness is diminishing. Both also continue with their respective weight gain and weight loss programmes. Food-wise, it's difficult to accommodate both ends of that spectrum simultaneously, but the health aspect is one of my top priorities. Sky begins to develop good friendships with Lily and Vincent, though she struggles with some basic aspects of 'being a child' – simply because she hasn't had the experience of childhood, or not one that most of us would recognise.

Before Avril's contraceptive implant appointment, I check in once more that everything is okay with Charlie and Maz for it to go ahead. They are entirely supportive of Avril's choice to take responsibility to manage her own body. Charlie even goes as far as to tell me that I have 'done well', which feels like high praise indeed. I'm still conscious that

I feel awkward about it all myself without explicit parental permission. It seems like a big deal, somehow. A big step in a young girl's life. At the same time, I also know that I will feel much happier when it is all done. I can't begin to imagine the repercussions if Avril were to get pregnant 'on my watch', as it were. What a responsibility. This is definitely the right way forward. I wonder what kind of conversations she has had with her mother on the subject, and how difficult they might have been for her.

While I'm reversing into a space in the car park of the doctors' surgery, Avril's phone goes.

She ignores it. It pings several times in rapid succession. She ignores those, too. I guess it must be Hanna. The phone rings again. Avril punches it off, crossly.

But as we are settling ourselves to sit down in the waiting room, Avril suddenly gets up and walks outside with the phone.

I look out of the window to see her pacing up and down. She hugs herself tightly with her free arm. The other has the phone pinned to the side of her head. She nods at times, chews her lip furiously. I can only guess what is being said. I prepare myself for what feels like the inevitable news that we will be driving home without the contraception.

Avril comes back into the waiting room, and to my joy, sits back down. The flumphing sound that comes from the faux leather bench as air is released should be disgusting but in this moment, signalling her return – and therefore her continued commitment to this – it's music to my ears.

'All right?'

She nods.

I let her be, not wanting to upset this fragile moment. I can imagine the internal conflict she is experiencing.

Her name is called.

'I'm waiting here, Avril. I'll be here when you come out. All this has to be your choice.'

I'm aware that Hanna could twist and turn this to suit her agenda, and although I am almost sure that Avril would like me to be in there with her, I can't do anything that might later be misconstrued.

She is only gone for a few minutes, but they are long ones for me.

I release a breath I didn't know I was holding when she appears back in the waiting room.

'All right?'

She nods. But she looks a little pale and her phone is pinging away. I want to wrench it from her hands and turn the damn thing off.

Instead I say, 'Shall we pop to the shop and get a drink?'

She doesn't speak, but follows me to the little kiosk. We stand in front of the drinks section by the sandwiches, and to my surprise, she selects a bottle of water. I offer no comment, but I'm delighted.

We've had an embargo on Josh visiting until her procedure is complete, and we need to wait another seven days to ensure full contraceptive protection, but I don't want to bring all that up and offer an invitation to Josh, in case it comes across as me suggesting that she should now go out and have intercourse. I'm certainly not condoning underage sex. How complicated it all is!

Back at the house Avril still doesn't look quite herself. I know that the implant procedure itself is painless, so I'm pretty sure this is a reaction to the pressure she is feeling from Hanna. 'I think I'm going to have a little lie down,' she says. I don't know whether she does it accidentally, or on purpose, but she leaves her phone on the kitchen table as she heads upstairs.

I move it to the garden room, out of the way. I return a moment later and slide it across slightly, so it nestles beneath a cushion. Somehow Hanna still manages to cast an ugly shadow, even though she isn't here. I have no doubt that there will be repercussions from what's happened today.

I report back to Charlie and Maz via email on the morning's events.

Maz phones a few minutes later to offer her congratulations. 'This is a major breakthrough, Louise.'

'The water as well as the implant,' I agree.

'Let's hope that it's the start of Avril breaking free from the hold that Hanna has on her.'

'She did really well today. I'm proud of her. I just wonder how Hanna will react. I wish I knew what her next move is going to be.'

At bedtime I notice that my make-up bag has been raided. It is open on my dressing table, and I know I had it zipped away in a drawer this morning. I can't be entirely sure, because it's a little while since I've had a good sort out, but I think that a blusher and a couple of eyeshadows are missing. Perhaps Avril is going to start taking more of an interest in her appearance. If that's the case, I'll take her shopping for some at the weekend. I wish she'd felt able to ask me if she could borrow some, but I don't want a confrontation; we are making such progress now.

The following morning the girls get ready for school as normal. Avril's phone is still lying underneath the cushion – she didn't come to retrieve it last night, but does ask for it this morning. I feel a moment's regret that I didn't think to leave an app running so that the battery would run down.

They get into the taxi and off they go – a much earlier start than my other children, who are still in various stages of getting up, since they only have a five-minute walk to their school. I wonder how big the taxi bill will be at the end of all this – enormous, I suspect. It's another services expenditure that might have been avoided with some forethought and common sense. It's not as if the girls were settled at their school when that decision was taken. Not my money, and not my decision. Step away, Louise.

My morning dash around the house reveals a pile of pinkish-stained towels in the corner of the bathroom. I've found worse, so I scoop them up with the laundry and think no more of it.

When the girls arrive home, I study their demeanour carefully to gauge how they are feeling. They are both quiet, but that is not unusual in itself.

'How're your arms feeling, Avril? All OK? No soreness?'

She nods and shrugs.

They both eat their snack quietly and don't engage with the chatter of the other children. Not unusual a few weeks ago, but it feels a little strained today. I try to stop the alarm bells from ringing in my head. Lloyd is getting ready to depart for a business trip. He does this quite often and it works fine for us; when he is away overnight, we tend to all watch a film together and eat popcorn and turn his absence into something fun.

Since the trip has been planned for a few weeks, and he will be away for a few nights, I've booked to take everyone out tomorrow night as a special treat. We will go for dinner at the Chinese Buffet, a local restaurant that does exactly as its name suggests. Nights out there are always a success, and so there is the wonderful joy of anticipation. All the children love the Chinese Buffet. There is something for everyone, even those who aren't particular fans of oriental cuisine, and there is such a convivial set-up for serving the food that it would be difficult not to enjoy it. Much hilarity always ensues as a result of the spinning lazy Susan that sits in the centre of each restaurant table. It's something for us all to look forward to.

The next morning I say goodbye to Lloyd, who has an early start for his trip and is sorry to be missing out on the Chinese meal.

'I'll make sure I call home at about dinnertime to talk to all the children. I should have arrived back at the hotel by then.'

He always tries to do this, making sure that he speaks to them around the mealtime, so that he is 'here' with us even if he isn't in the room.

'Save me a portion of Chinese Buffet,' he jokes. 'And try not to have too much fun without me!' He is whistling as he heads off to the airport.

I climb upstairs to Sky and Avril's rooms, and give a quick tap on each of their doors.

'Wakey wakey, time to get up,' I call out cheerfully.

I usually hear a groan or answer of some sort, and when I get nothing at all from either I open the door to Sky's room and look in. Sky is buried beneath her bedding. I gently pull the duvet off her head.

She yanks it back forcefully and hides.

'What's all this about? It's time to get up.'

She ignores me, and I sense that this is not a playful resistance.

'Sky, it's time for breakfast, and we have pancakes.'

Nothing.

I walk back to Avril's room, knock again and open her door. She is lying in bed with her headphones on.

'Avril, love, it's time for school. Time to get up now and get ready.'

She ignores me completely. There is no acknowledgement that I am even in the room. I feel a mutiny brewing.

If only I'd known what was to come.

I get the others up and sort out their breakfasts. I keep going back up to the girls' rooms to rouse them. Not even the mention of food and chocolate spread moves Sky.

'Right, girls. This has got out of hand. The taxi is here, waiting.'

I am becoming increasingly frustrated.

'Did you hear me? The taxi is outside. You need to be in it.'

Still nothing.

'Listen, this isn't funny. I have appointments today. The dentist was a one-off. You can't stay at home today.'

The penny drops. I get it. This is Hanna's protest. She is using the children to punish me for the dentist and the contraceptive implant.

I run out to the taxi and apologise to the driver. There's no point in keeping him waiting; this is evidently not going to be easily resolved.

Back in Avril's room I ask her to get up again. 'I've sent the taxi away, which doesn't mean that you're not going. It means that I am going to have to take you both in myself. I've got a busy day, and this isn't ideal.' Which is something of an understatement, but I don't want to lose my temper.

I go and see Sky as Jackson begins calling out for his PE shorts.

'They're on the clothes horse in the garden room. Right-hand side.'

Sky is still pretending to not hear me. I march over to her bed and pull off the duvet. 'You have to get up. I'm going to drive you to school myself.'

Downstairs, the other children are curious to know what's happening.

'I'm not sure,' I say, wearily.

'Avril was talking to her mum for hours last night,' Jackson says. 'I could hear her.'

It doesn't surprise me, but it's such a shame, especially after all the progress we've made with Avril taking responsibility for her contraception and resisting the influence of her mother.

I say goodbye to Jackson, Vincent and Lily, and do my best to suggest that nothing is wrong, continuing to hide my brewing anger and frustration as well as I can.

A tough reality for me, as a foster carer, is being caught in the crossfire when parents are prepared to use their children as weapons to fight their wars. You hear about separated parents using their children to get at each other. I understand that to a point, particularly when there is a complicated history and complex emotions are being played out. When it does happen, it's unfortunate, but doesn't usually feel personal. In this case, it really does. I'm well and truly caught in the crossfire, even though I have no relationship with Hanna other than that I responded to their referral as a foster carer. I mentally delete the words 'made the mistake of' as I think about this. Although it is directed towards me, clearly, I also recognise that this fight is part of Hanna's anger and frustration about things she is unable to control in her own life. It becomes an illustration of the way that people just transfer their emotional stuff on to others because they are angry. It probably explains much of the abuse and bullying that goes on in life. There is a reason – we just don't always see it. I have no desire to fight with a woman I don't know. I have also, as I almost inevitably do, come to care deeply about what happens to Sky and Avril.

Deep breath.

I go back upstairs where I find Sky now underneath her bed, barricaded in with the duvet.

'Come on, Sky. Seriously. Get up and stop this. We need to get you to school.'

She starts screaming.

Oh no, here we go. The events of 'the incident' night come back in a flash.

I walk over to the window and close it – just to try to keep the decibels of screams somewhat contained in the house.

Another deep breath.

I walk to Avril's room, where I knock first and then open the door. She is sitting on her bed, gaming. She refuses to look at me or engage in any way. It is like I have ceased to exist for her.

I go back to Sky's room. She is still screaming. I lift the bed off and away from her, placing it on its side against the wall. I stand in front of it so she has lost her shelter. I know that these are not the 'correct' actions. I know that I need to handle this better. But all the courses and training fly out of the window when you have a child behaving so irrationally like this. And I genuinely have to be somewhere for work today. I am meeting my new editor, and was hoping to make a good impression.

But then they know this, don't they? A light-bulb moment. Avril has looked in my diary, of course.

Another deep breath.

I need to think differently. I write about children with or in trauma. I'm supposed to be someone who has answers to this sort of thing. I make a conscious decision to approach this differently.

I pull the bed to a safe place.

'Okay, Sky, you stay there. I'm off to carry on with my work.' My voice is calm. Happy. Sing-song. As though I don't have a care in the world.

I walk up to Avril's door. 'Just making breakfast if you want it.'

Again my voice is calm, and the tone is light and sing-song. And with the pretence, all the agitation I felt a few moments before genuinely does begin to evaporate.

I leave them to it. I call my editor and tell her what's going on – or an abbreviated version, at least. I apologise and explain that for the time being I can't leave.

She is lovely and supportive – and also fascinated by the turn events have taken today. We reschedule our meeting for a few days' time. I go into my studio, where I phone the school and explain to them what's going on and why Sky and Avril won't be making an appearance today. I email the social workers. I start the daily log.

I can't leave the girls alone to take the dogs for a walk so they miss out, though I play with them in the garden and laugh as they run round and round – which of course reminds me of the 'knickers' day.

I put the washing on. I turn the radio on. I carry on. What else can I do?

I keep an ear out to see what they're up to; if they go to each other's rooms.

After a little while, Avril does indeed do this. I can hear what's being said from a certain place at the bottom of the stairs.

'Sky? Hanna said we need to wreck our rooms.' She runs back to her room.

Oh excellent. I knew I was in for a treat.

I walk straight up the stairs. 'First one dressed gets the biggest McDonald's meal – with extra ice cream.'

Poor Sky doesn't know what to do. I know usually she cannot resist an offer like that, but she is well and truly caught between the hold of Hanna – the authority of her mum – and me and my treat.

I trip away back down the stairs with my faux-happy cheer. But I have everything crossed, desperately hoping that this works.

I wait and wait. They've both been awake in their rooms since before seven o'clock. It's now moving towards midday. I start frying some bacon, knowing that both girls love bacon sandwiches.

I sing. I put the vacuum cleaner round the rooms. I answer the phone. I play loud music. As I knew they must sooner or later, the tummy rumbles get to them. Sky comes down. That winning beam of a smile is gone, but she sits at the table.

'There you are,' I say. 'Would you like some lunch?'

She nods.

I call up to Avril. 'Bacon sandwich waiting for you in the kitchen!'

She too appears.

I don't speak other than to say hello.

While they eat, I do a slightly devious thing. I make a pretend phone call to cancel a meeting I have tomorrow,

179

strongly suspecting that Avril has probably screenshot my diary. It usually sits open on my desk, but it will have a new home after today. I feel slightly silly talking to no one about rescheduling, but figure that way they can't hold me to ransom. My game plan here is to sit tight. If I take everything in my stride then that will take the wind out of Hanna's sails and her campaign will lose momentum.

I cancel the Chinese Buffet – for real. I worry about how I'll explain that to the others later. I'll make it up to them, but there's no way we're going out tonight after the shenanigans these two have pulled this morning.

I return to updating the log and leave the girls alone, but early in the afternoon I notice that they have gone up to Avril's room and have shut the door. I knock on the door and push it open halfway, giving them a gentle smile and a firm nod as I do.

I take a bundle of clean washing into our room and sit down for a moment on the bed behind the door. It enables me to hear Sky talking on the telephone – definitely to her mother, because I hear her say, 'Sorry, Hanna' several times.

I've got used to the references to 'Hanna' rather than 'Mum' by now, but it still jars sometimes. When I was growing up in Oxford in the 1970s, I remember children at my school that called their parents by their first names. It always felt a little contrived. They were usually the children of academics, and it seemed to be quite a trend. I wonder why. Perhaps as a parent, having your child refer to you by your name somehow relinquishes you of the toil of parenting, as if you're waiting to be able to talk to a fully formed adult. But what do I know?

I sit and listen with interest. They talk quietly, but my ears are picking up their conversation. I get a sense that the girls are being told what to do in a series of explicit instructions. After each short pause this end, a 'Yes, Hanna' follows.

I hear Avril say, 'No, she isn't going tomorrow now.'

It gives me no pleasure to discover that I was right: Hanna is trying to cause maximum disruption to our lives, or at least to my life. Once again, although I try to rationalise it and remind myself of Hanna's side of things, it can't help but feel very personal.

I have no idea what it is that they are plotting, and they don't repeat any of the instructions they receive back. I wait a bit longer before moving back downstairs to my studio. I haven't left my laptop out since I felt suspicion in the first few days after the girls arrived. It is a pain to have to keep getting it out and set up, but I feel slightly less vulnerable that way and it's becoming a habit now. I add a little more to my logs and send an updated email to the social workers. I want their advice about what to do if this happens again tomorrow, which I think it might.

I get on and do some more work in my studio. Now that I am not meeting my editor, I can get on with some illustrations that need attention, and an article I'm writing about mindfulness: all about the importance of accepting but simultaneously letting go of negative thoughts and emotions, and how to practise that successfully.

Oh, the irony.

Chapter Twenty

Just as the other children come home from school, Maz calls.

'After reading your emails and the log, I contacted Charlie. He's spoken to Hanna directly this afternoon. You'll like this: apparently Hanna knows nothing at all about the behaviour of the girls today, and is deeply hurt by any accusation that she might be the cause of it. Actually, she's relieved that you are looking after her daughters so well, apparently.'

'Yeah, right!' I snort.

I don't think either of us believe that. But – mindfulness. I decide to get into a zone where nothing, but nothing, can wind me up. Hanna can't do anything to me that will stress me or make me angry. I will simply not allow myself to become angry. My deep breathing is coming along a treat.

'So, if the girls do another protest like that in the morning, just leave them to it. Don't make them breakfast; in fact, don't go anywhere near them. Leave them to let the fire go out of their actions.'

'Yes, good. I totally agree.'

If there's one thing I do know, it's that when a child is acting up it's best to remove the audience, so that's what we'll do.

I feel better having Maz onside and offering advice.

I hum my way through cooking dinner for the children. Jackson sits up on the kitchen unit near the cooker, one eye on what I'm doing because he likes cooking himself, and one eye on the others as they share their stories about the day.

'So, did they end up going to school?' Lily asks.

'No. Not today. No, they didn't.' I try to sound as neutral as I can.

There is a chorus of disapproval and a series of, 'Well, that's not fair!'

I don't really want to engage, so give a look that I hope says, 'Really?' to end the discussion.

When I call the girls down for dinner there is no answer, not even from Sky, who is usually in the kitchen circling before I've even had a chance to prepare the table.

I set the plates for five, as though everything is normal. But they don't come down. Lloyd calls for his promised chat with the children.

When I say hello, he warns, 'Don't put it on speakerphone.'

'Why?'

'Are you sitting down? How's the restaurant?'

'We're not there. Long story, mostly involving Tweedledum and Tweedledee. I'll tell you later.'

He sighs. 'Right. Well, you're not going to like this either.'

My heart sinks.

'Brace yourself. She's posted every page from your logs and highlighted certain sections, calling them lies.'

'*What?*'

'It gets worse.'

'It can't, but go on.'

'She's accused you of encouraging Avril to have sex by putting her on the pill.'

'You are joking,' I say, knowing that he isn't.

'Is that Dad? Can we talk to him?' Jackson says.

I raise a delaying hand.

'She has a picture of you up there, too. I think Avril must have screenshot one of your publicity shots.'

'So I'm named and linked with the documents?'

'Yep.'

'Private, confidential documents that she shouldn't have any access to? That are, in fact, stored on my password-protected laptop?'

'Yep.'

'Jesus.'

There is a long pause while I try and work out what to think, what to feel. Mindfulness is taking a backseat right now.

'Louise, are you OK?'

'I don't know what to say.'

'I know. It's diabolical. But is that Jackson I can hear? Better let me talk to the kids, while you digest that.'

'OK, guys, Dad's here. You're going on speakerphone,' I say cheerfully, as though everything is normal and fine. But inside I am stressed to the max.

She's won.

Chapter Twenty-One

The girls still don't come down from their bedrooms.

This has gone beyond making some kind of point now. They've been there for hours and it is suspiciously quiet. I don't quite know what to do. I guess they'll appear when they're hungry, but I'm surprised this hasn't happened already – especially for Sky.

Part of me doesn't want to get online and look, but I'm drawn to my laptop to see Lloyd's news for myself. It's as bad – no, worse – than he described.

Maz answers straight away when I call.

'I've heard,' she says, when I start ranting down the phone.

'So, when can we get it taken down?'

She sighs. 'We can't ask her to take it down, I'm afraid.'

'Why?' I screech, through gritted teeth.

'Well, because her solicitor gave it to her. And it wasn't marked as confidential. I'm sorry, Louise.'

'But she's shared it with so many people! And those pictures!'

The publication of my logs and the accusation of being a liar isn't the worst thing about Hanna's post. The reason I'm so alarmed is that there are pictures of the girls, alongside the documents, and the images are horrific. Both children appear with darkened patches of skin, like deep bruises, across their faces. Faces that are tear-stained and accompanied by expressions of torment. Except that, of course, they are not real. Both appear with red eyes and made-up, downcast faces. That explains the stained towels in their bathroom and the disappearance of my eyeshadow.

Avril and Sky are Hanna's children and she can choose to post their pictures online, authentic or not. I can't, of course, because I am just the foster carer.

'Are you looking at this? More stuff's going up!'

Other pictures appear when we refresh the page, of our bathroom and my studio. I feel strangely exposed. It's more invasive than the documents, almost. And then there are nasty comments about my work: *Shit drawings.* Ouch!

I also notice all the shares her post has already had on Facebook. This may be the closest I have come to going viral. Perhaps the most upsetting thing is the comments beneath the post. They are vile.

Child thief.

Abuser.

Child catcher.

'Have you seen what they are saying about me? I'm calling the police.'

'I wish there was something I could do to help, but there's nothing. I'm so sorry, Louise.'

It feels a little bit like being burgled. I feel totally violated. Hanna is winning, but it's a battle I didn't sign up for, and I don't have any armour or any weapons. This is part of her war against authority and the world.

Lloyd calls me back. He's still angry but has calmed down a little. I guess he has talked to his colleagues. He works with a bunch of people that he is very close to, some of whom have become family friends. They are all very sensible, rational people and have probably already helped him to reach the conclusion, as I have deep down, that there really is nothing we can do. I fill him in on the stand-off that is developing.

'It's not good, Louise. I wish I was there to do something.'

But what exactly to do, with or without Lloyd?

I don't want to see the girls at all, but know that it is time to dig deep. Hanna will be pulling the strings to this puppet show, ready to control the next scene. I need to stop that from happening. I need to surprise her.

When I look at the clock it's only six o'clock. Still early. The children have already returned to the kitchen once, complaining that they are still hungry. Now Lily pops her head around the door and makes big eyes at me.

A little plan is forming. I make a suggestion. 'Only if the girls want to, though, because I can't leave anyone here alone, but we could all go out to the Italian ice cream parlour.'

'Yesss!' Lily squeals. The sound is accompanied by a little air punch as she goes off to enlist the help of Vincent. He doesn't need much persuading that this is an amazing idea and the best offer he's going to get this evening. They tear along the hallway to find Sky, who is not in her own room, but in with Avril, door shut.

They knock and barge in with no qualms. 'Come on you two! Let's go to the ice cream parlour!'

Sky is out of the room and putting on her shoes and coat within a second.

Meanwhile, Jackson walks by Avril's door. 'Trust me. The honeycomb's amazing.'

I think Avril wants to be friends with Jackson. She wants to belong, even if it's only just a little. Jackson gets this intuitively. He is an experienced foster sibling, and his words do the trick.

Avril slides off the bed and comes downstairs. She is literally dragging her feet, but they are moving in my direction.

I greet them with a huge smile. 'Who's going in the front seat of the car?'

We drive along the motorway and the electro-popping rhythms of Icona Pop come on the radio. The beat is so strong that feet tap and heads move in time to it.

'Come on,' I say, 'we don't care, and we love it, don't we? All together!'

I turn the volume right up and we all start singing. Sky cracks straight away and picks up the lyrics. Avril takes slightly longer, but after the first chorus, joins in with fist pumps and singing. We roar down the motorway, children singing – or shouting – at the top of their voices.

I win this round.

Chapter Twenty-Two

Sky is quiet this morning when she comes down for breakfast, not beaming as she usually does. While the other children are getting ready for school, she is looking a little bit, well, what I can only describe as 'shifty'. It's a look that I have come to associate much more with Avril than with her.

'Are you all right, Sky?' I ask. 'Are you feeling okay?'

She nods.

'Ready for breakfast?'

She pulls up a chair.

'We'll have to be quick because the taxi will be here any minute. How would you like a waffle?'

Again, she nods.

I pour half a glass of orange juice out and pass it to her while the waffle toasts.

I call up to Avril. 'Just doing a waffle for Sky – would you like one for breakfast, too?'

No answer.

I keep calling. 'Avril? Avril? Time to come down for breakfast.'

My phone pings. It's Hanna – who else?

Avril doesn't feel well.

I put Sky's waffle on a plate and quickly head upstairs.

'Avril? Are you okay in there?' I knock a couple of times on her door before opening it. She is sitting up in bed with her headphones on, playing a game on her Xbox.

'Avril? Are you okay?'

She doesn't look away from her game. 'I have a temperature. I've been sick and my tummy is…' She makes a face to finish the sentence.

Great. Not sick enough to stop concentrating on the mobs spawning in her house, or whatever it is she's doing in that bloody game. The irony is not lost on me. Hanna has given her all the cues to avoid going to school for at least a few days. The policy is that students need to be 48 hours clear after any stomach upset.

I offer a conciliatory smile, but I'm annoyed. There's nothing wrong with that child, but I can't leave her. I'm busy today. I have errands to run and people to see. But I have no doubt that Hanna knows that – knows my exact timetable, in fact.

The taxi arrives and I lead Sky outside to make sure she gets in safely. But there is another hitch that I haven't foreseen.

'I can't take her unless she has an escort, because she's too young. Normally her sister is with her, so it's fine, but I won't be able to take her on her own,' the taxi driver explains.

Great, I say to myself again. I have them both here all day once more.

The other children have packed their school bags and are in the final stages of their departure.

Jackson raises an eyebrow when Sky comes back in with me and the taxi retreats into the distance. 'Are they staying at home *again*?'

And the plot thickens, or the knife twists, or something. Hanna is so good at this. She knows that the other children will become resentful of the special treatment her daughters seem to be getting.

What I guess is that Hanna is trying to break the place-ment down and have her children moved. If they go to another placement she will do it again – to demonstrate that there was nothing wrong with her parenting and the system is failing her children. She's a piece of work. I don't think she cares if the children are settled, happy and becoming healthy – this is about her fight against something bigger, something more important to her than her own family.

But my family *is* important to me, and I can't have dissent within the ranks.

I roll my eyes to the children. 'I know, I know. It's just circumstances. I'm stuck. I can't send them to school because Sky can't be in a taxi on her own and Avril is ill.' I can't resist adding, 'apparently,' after a moment's pause.

They go on moaning about foster children and all the problems they bring.

'Anyone would think that the normal rules didn't apply.'

Lily is the most vociferous on the subject, which makes me smile. After all, she is a foster child herself.

I turn to Sky. 'You may as well put your play clothes on. Make sure that you fold your uniform up and put it on the chair ready for tomorrow.'

I clear up the kitchen and feel that sinking feeling that comes with the knowledge that my day is disappearing. I have some deadlines coming up that I need to be ready for, but the chances of achieving them are becoming slimmer all the time. These girls have already put me a long way behind.

I call Maz and leave a message for her about the girls' absence today.

I email Charlie with the details too, remembering to copy Maz in. Every action like this creates more work. It's work that I wouldn't mind at all if Avril really were ill, but I'm certain that she's not. Tummy pain didn't seem to be a problem when she was tucking into the ice cream last night. Why can't Hanna understand that her children's education needs to be prioritised above her spiteful vendetta against me?

I write my logs, mindful that I don't say what I really think about the situation, but report only the facts. It is important to ensure that they are nothing other than bland, bland, bland. Who knows what will appear online next? I was never told that the birth parents' solicitor would give a copy of my logs to Hanna. I feel deeply uncomfortable – and bullied. I have to write all this stuff down, now with no assurance of its confidentiality – and worse, its likely publication.

I want to pursue the logs incident further with Maz, because it seems unfair on a number of counts. We are told to keep detailed logs, especially with a new placement. We are told to write down as much detail as possible, and encouraged to record the small stuff of daily activities: keeping track of meals, family activities, and even sports and clubs attendance. Well, there hasn't been a great deal of that. But certainly any 'incidents', which counts as anything that is even slightly unusual in some way – like refusing to go to school, refusing to eat, or demonstrating 'non-compliant' behaviour. These two have certainly kept me busy in that department.

I hesitate for a moment, before adding the photos from my phone of the disturbing drawings under the bed that Sky created.

Next it's time to start the bedroom clear-ups. I walk straight past the door to Avril's room, taking on Jackson's room at the top of the house first: shaking out the duvet and picking up anything on the floor, any remaining washing. I do the same for Lily and Vincent, then finally go into Sky's room.

I can't believe my eyes.

She has drawn in Sharpie on every surface and piece of furniture. She has drawn all over the walls. She has drawn on the rugs and on the painted floorboards. Every surface is ruined, marked, damaged, destroyed. The whole place is a scribbled mess. It looks like a poor imitation of the graffiti that once covered the Berlin Wall.

I can't stop the sharp intake of breath – it's a visceral reaction to this vandalism.

The artist herself is standing behind me, still with pen in hand. Her eyes are full of tears. Panic fills her features. She throws herself into the corner of the room and turns into a ball.

She begins to scream, 'Don't hurt me! Please don't hurt me!'

I take a deep breath.

I don't have to turn to know that Avril is outside the door holding up her phone.

I close the door gently, leaving Avril behind it on the other side.

Sky is in a terrible state. Tears pour down her face, snot hangs from her nose. I am struck most by how wide her eyes seem. Normally they are small, buried deep in her swollen face, but right now they are wide and scared.

I sit down as near to her as I can without frightening her more. 'I know you didn't want to do this, Sky, I do. It's okay.'

She tilts her head away from me and looks towards the window. She can't look me in the eye, but just repeats over and over, 'I'm sorry, Louise, I'm sorry, Louise, I'm sorry, Louise.' Even the action of saying those words is working her up more. The words become indistinguishable from one another. 'I'msorryLouiseI'msorryLouise.'

I lift my arm to wipe a tear from my eye, and she instantly flinches away and curls up to protect herself. I have seen enough to understand what this child must have been experiencing. I move back so that she doesn't feel threatened, but stay for a while longer making reassuring noises.

'It's okay, Sky, it's okay. I promise. We can fix this; there is nothing here that can't be sorted out. This room needed to be redecorated anyway.'

It doesn't: we finished redecorating it just before the girls arrived, and most of the furniture is new. Not to mention the work that went into repainting those floorboards. They alone will present a challenge, but she has no need to know that.

This child is in trauma – total trauma. She is so conflicted. I think I despise Hanna for doing this to her.

Eventually she settles down. When the sobs have subsided to their intermittent shuddering aftermath, I help her off the floor. She doesn't resist my hand like she normally does. I sit her on the bed and position myself there next to her. I put my arm around her shoulder and gently pull her in.

Tears still spill from her eyes, as if she has an endless supply. The skin around them looks puffier, if that's possible, and sore with redness. I pull her on to my lap. She willingly comes. I put both arms around her swollen body and begin to rock back and forth like I did with the boys when they were younger, and still do with Lily when she is upset. This little girl has never had the most basic acts of love bestowed upon her. She has been living in the crossfire of someone else's war with the world. She leans close against me. I stroke her hair and place my chin softly on the top of her head. We rock there together until the tears finally fade.

When we pull apart, she looks exhausted.

'You get into bed with Zebra and I'll get you a drink.'

I pull the cover up over this hurt little girl.

Chapter Twenty-Three

I half expect Avril to be waiting in the same position outside the door, but she is back in her room. I can hear the muffled sounds of conversation. She is talking to Hanna.

Not for much longer, she isn't.

I walk in, grab the phone and speak to Hanna myself.

'You can listen to me, now. I think, Hanna, what you did today is the lowest of the low. If you could only see the state your youngest child is in, it might help you to understand.'

I need to feel that my home is mine and that she is not dominating it from a stupid phone, miles away and unreachable.

I pause only to snatch a breath. 'You are manipulative and cruel, do you hear me? You use your children like pawns in your fight against a system. A system that, actually, if you stopped and thought about it, is funding you and actually trying to help you. Why can't you get that into your head?'

I don't give her a chance to answer.

'Tell me, what would you do, Hanna, if there was no NHS, or benefits didn't exist?' I don't really know quite what I am saying, and I certainly don't hold back now that I've got the chance to vent. Again, I don't give her a chance to answer.

'You'd be dead, that's what would happen.'

I'm angry, and something in me has been completely unleashed, just as it was for Sky. I am angry at Hanna for using her children – at the cost of their health and happiness. It seems to me an utterly despicable thing to do.

Avril sits down heavily on her bed, stunned.

'And if you think you're going to bring me and my family down to your sick level, you can think on. You don't matter, do you hear me? I'm here to look after your children.'

I look directly at Avril. 'And if they don't want that then they can go, but I know for a fact that Sky wants to be here, and *needs* to be here. It's the best place for her.'

A beat.

'Goodbye,' I say, in a tone that Anne Robinson, ridding contestants on *The Weakest Link,* would have been proud of. But this is no game show.

The call is ended, but I'm not done. I look at Avril. 'This phone is now confiscated,' I announce, and walk out of the room.

I'm shaking as I pick up my own phone to call Maz and fill her in, but I am no longer feeling like the victim.

Hanna is not doing this to *us* in our own home, and how dare she do this to her children? Today's outburst has reminded me just how young and vulnerable Sky is, and how damaging it is for her to be manipulated in this way. Avril is going to have to think about what she wants and come to her own decision. There are now terms attached to this placement, terms that I have just invented, and I am not in the mood for silliness from Charlie or Claire. Just let them try.

Next I talk to Lloyd. He's furious about the vandalised room, but it doesn't take me long to bring him round to see that it's not Sky's fault.

'Honestly, Lloyd. If you could just have seen how scared she was. It's diabolical what Hanna has done to these girls.'

By the time the children come home from school, I have cooked a lovely dinner, and for pudding distribute what feels like an endless supply of pancakes with chocolate sauce and maple syrup. Avril deigns to join us for the meal.

'Can I have my phone back, please?'

'No, not tonight. I need a night off from Hanna, and frankly, so do you.'

The next morning I continue with my no-nonsense approach. Both girls are dressed and ready for school. Avril is sullen, and I ignore all requests for her to be given her phone back.

'Not yet. Maybe later. We'll see.'

I have already decided that she can have it later, but in good time: a day without Hanna's constant pestering and manipulating will do her good, and perhaps allow peace to reign in the household once more.

They get into the taxi, Avril still alternating between protesting and begging. It's the same taxi driver as yesterday, and he gives me a congratulatory nod when he hears me tell her a final time that she can't have the phone yet. He doesn't know the half of it. I see the other children off (who are much happier that the girls are back at school too).

I don't even get as far as the morning laundry and bed dash, but head straight to write up the logs while everything is still fresh and clear in my mind.

I make the mistake of clicking on an email from Charlie.

I'm afraid I have to tell you that Hanna has made a formal complaint against you for not using the full clothing allowance on Avril. Apparently she desperately needs new clothes.

Yep. Here we go. The only sadness is that I am not surprised in the slightest. I think about the shopping trip I took with Avril when she was taking care of her appearance and trying to impress Josh. Though now that I think about it, she hasn't mentioned him for a while now. Perhaps they've split up. It's unlikely that she would announce it, I suppose. I take a deep breath and email back, cc'ing Maz.

Thank you for your email.

(I'm trying my hardest to be polite.)

It's interesting to hear that, Charlie.

Perhaps it would help to know that I'm still waiting for money I spent upfront buying both girls new clothes when they arrived with nothing clean to wear; the money I then spent kitting both girls out with three sets of new clothes each, plus new school uniforms including shoes and trainers, school bags and PE kits. With the night clothes, underwear and dressing gowns, the total expenditure currently sits at around £600.

I'm currently still waiting for the £40 per month teenagers' clothing allowance which is in arrears, so I estimate at least another three months until we have to spend any more money.

I'll attach the scanned receipts that I sent last month again, but according to the Egress secure email system they were received into your mailbox.

I wonder if he can tell that I am typing through gritted teeth.

I receive a swift reply from Charlie.

Thank you for letting me know.

Nothing more.

Fine. I didn't expect a round of applause.

I tell myself that Lloyd gets home tomorrow, which means I only have to spend one more night alone with the children. I usually enjoy the times when Lloyd's away, in the nicest possible way. We tend to band together as a little tribe, and touchingly, the boys like snuggling on the sofa in their onesies. This time, though, he can't come home soon enough.

I manage to get a lot of work done. The fact that I'm fired up emotionally translates into my artwork, and I actually have a very productive day in the studio. It's at the expense of housework and shopping, but I can quickly pop out before the children get home and grab some essentials. The main shopping can wait.

My three arrive in a clump, and, as ever, they are hungry and thirsty. They throw their bags and coats on to the floor. I moan and pick it all up. It's a well-worn routine and we all know our cues. They settle down to games and television before dinner, while I go through their homework and call them into the kitchen one at a time so I can help and supervise. Apart from maths, where I'm not ashamed to admit that I'm definitely in a supervisory rather than a helping capacity. I was diagnosed with dyscalculia and dyslexia when I was a young adult – which explained why I struggled so much and was called stupid, and consequently hated school.

Thankfully the children haven't inherited these tendencies, nor have they rubbed off on Lily. And I'm very glad about that. If I even attempt to help them with a mathematical problem, I would likely only succeed in helping them lose marks. Lloyd is good for maths. We Skype him to help Vincent work on a few calculations. Happily, he has finished work for the day and has arrived back in his hotel room. I'm tempted to ask him to see if he can change flights and come back tonight, but I resist. I can do this. Calculations complete, Vincent is gone like the wind back to his computer game, which leaves me time to carry on talking to Lloyd. I potter about the kitchen preparing dinner and give him the latest updates, telling him about Charlie's 'complaint' email. He splutters into his wine glass and produces a number of swear words. I push the door to.

There are no children in the room, but I don't want any of this to carry.

'Is it worth it?' he asks. 'We have to face the fact that she simply isn't going to give up. This isn't going to get any easier.'

'True. I think I've arrived at that conclusion, too. But we do at least have enough evidence now to show the pattern in her behaviour, and the girls' behaviour.'

'It's a pattern that's unsustainable, as far as I'm concerned.'

I hear their taxi pull up outside, bringing them back from school.

'Okay, they're here. Gotta go.'

'Call me if anything else happens.'

I go to meet them at the front door. Sky seems happier than she did this morning, but still not quite herself. She doesn't greet me with that winning, beaming smile I have grown so fond of. Maybe the car journey was unpleasant. It's a long way and sometimes taxis can have a certain cloying artificial air freshener smell, or the heating can be on too high.

Out comes Avril, with a pronounced limp. The taxi driver has to help her by holding her bag and closing the door behind her.

'Avril. What's happened to you?'

'I've broken my ankle,' she says, hobbling forward towards the house, but clearly able to weight-bear.

I avoid forming a raised eyebrow. 'You mean you've sprained it?'

She looks sheepish.

'Come on in,' I say, reaching to hold her elbow. She pulls away. These girls really are deeply uncomfortable about touch.

'Bye,' I say to the taxi driver as he hands me her things. 'Thanks for your help.'

I wait patiently as she hobbles indoors. It's not terrifically convincing – she seems to shift weight distribution from leg to leg fairly arbitrarily – but it wouldn't be helpful to point this out.

'Dinner's nearly ready; it'll be another half an hour.'

Sky has gone ahead to find Lily. I head towards the kitchen, but hang back and watch Avril climb up the stairs. She manages perfectly well: no limping.

My phone rings. It's Charlie.

'Good afternoon, Louise. Hanna is insisting that you take Avril to the hospital.'

'Oh, and why would that be?' I say. It doesn't occur to me straight away to wonder how Avril has communicated with Hanna without her phone. 'She's absolutely fine. She can't decide which leg is hurting her the most, and I've just watched her walk up the stairs.'

'Are you a doctor?' he says. 'You have to take her. If it later turned out that there was anything wrong, you know we'd be in deep trouble.'

'We?'

He ignores my comment.

I get the table ready and call Avril down. The others are already seated, cutlery poised to dig in. She runs to the landing but when she sees me at the foot of the stairs, the limp is suddenly back.

She's been working on the performance, and has now added in a wincing face and a continual rubbing of her shin. It was her ankle earlier.

'Dinner,' I say in a tone that suggests I'm not in the mood to argue.

I can't leave the other children home alone, and it's too short notice to get a babysitter, so I will have to take all of them to the Accident & Emergency Centre at the hospital – which is a good 45-minute drive away. What fun. I clear up the table, sort the children out, text Lloyd and get them all into the car. I make sure that Jackson sits in the front with me. Avril will have to fold her legs behind our seats. It doesn't seem too problematic for her to manage that.

Now I do stop to consider, briefly, what means Hanna has used to communicate with Avril given that I have her phone, but I don't spend too much time thinking about it. I've been here before, a number of times. One child I looked after had five phones which he used on rotation. I guess Hanna was not going to take the risk of breaking communication, so no doubt there would have been back-up phones stashed into Avril's bag or trousers when she arrived.

I park the car in a spot that lies a good way away from the A&E building. I want to observe Avril's walking capabilities properly, over a decent distance. She ups the drama even more now, and we have pretend crying at one point, though she isn't enough of an actress to manage actual tears.

In the waiting room Sky sits tight with the others, saying nothing. I notice that she doesn't offer her sister any consolation.

I sign in at the reception desk where the member of staff is busying herself wiping down a little whiteboard that sits on top of the desk – changing the '2' to a '3' so that it now reads: WAITING TIME IS APPROXIMATELY 3 HOURS.

I could scream.

Meanwhile, out comes the second phone. Avril takes a photo of me standing next to the board. No doubt it will be sent to Hanna, who must be laughing her head off, settled in her own home for the evening – while my night's been sideways bulldozed.

I had the foresight to grab drinks and snacks from home, which is just as well because the dispensing machine in the waiting room is broken.

'I'm just going outside for a bit of fresh air,' Avril announces.

I watch her limp to the double glass sliding door. I shift my seat and watch her out of the window. She thinks she's pretty cool, but clearly doesn't know that I can see her. As she chats on the phone she is very relaxed. No sign of any wincing now. She has one hand on the lamp post and swings round it, then she crosses the road to sit at the bus stop. She swings both legs on the seat with no trouble whatsoever. Next she heads towards the helipad and actually runs and skips.

I take it all in. What exactly does she think she's going to achieve here?

The children get bored and irritable, of course. But Hanna would know that too, wouldn't she? No doubt that is giving her great delight, too.

Eventually Avril comes back in. I sit with my arms folded, looking at her. I just keep looking and say nothing.

Two hours pass. We watch entire scenes take place in that waiting room that wouldn't be out of place in an episode of *EastEnders*. Many people come and go, all in far more dramatic states of injury and suffering than our Avril. At one point a black-and-white cat appears and stretches out on the reception desk, clearly known to the staff.

Sky and Lily think this is amazing.

'Do you think he's the doctor?' Lily giggles.

We call him Doctor Mog, and his antics keep us entertained for the final hour and more.

Eventually Avril is called.

'Okay – I need the rest of you to sit still and wait here. Doctor Mog has got his eye on you.'

I have a quick chat with the reception staff, who also agree to keep an eye out while we are being seen. I'm not going to miss this.

Avril hobbles behind the doctor, who leads us into a curtained cubicle. She has a white Cruella de Vil-style streak in her hair, and somehow isn't dissimilar to Doctor Mog.

Avril gets herself up on to the bed, taking deep breaths as if she is gulping for air.

The doctor feels her ankle and looks at the paperwork, then at me.

'Are you her mother?'

'No,' I say quickly. 'No, no. I'm Avril's foster carer.'

Dr Cruella Mog doesn't beat about the bush.

'There's absolutely nothing wrong with your ankle, Avril. No swelling, nothing. You've wasted your foster mum's time, not to mention mine.'

She looks at both of us again, then narrows her eyes. 'Is there any particular reason why you wanted to pretend that your ankle was hurt?'

Avril hangs her head and refuses to make eye contact.

Dr Cruella is evidently a smart woman and has no doubt seen this sort of thing before. She hands me the paperwork back with a tight-lipped smile.

'Enjoy the rest of your evening.'

Avril walks back to the car dragging her feet, but not because of any limp now. I drive home feeling much better. We did the 'right' thing, and Avril's deception was discovered. Perhaps some good can come out of this wasted evening, after all. The long drive gives me more time to think, and a plan forms.

Sky will have no chance to thrive here with us as long as Hanna and Avril continue to peck away at her.

But at the same time I know that social workers don't like splitting up siblings, and with very good reason. I resolve to write it all up in my logs, which I guess Hanna's solicitor will pass on to Hanna as before. I resign myself to the fact that they may well appear on the internet again. But that will not stop me from explaining the harm Avril's and Hanna's manipulation is doing to little Sky. We will have to give notice on the placements. In my heart I want to keep Sky with us. I know that she has made progress, that different aspects of her behaviour have changed, and that she is healthier and happier when she is here with us.

Avril cannot stay with us any longer, it's as simple as that. I email Charlie.

We don't feel that we are able to fully meet Avril's needs. He will understand the code: children's social care talk for *this really isn't working*.

Chapter Twenty-Four

When I finally stop to think about it all, I realise that I haven't noticed how much Hanna's antics have taken their toll.

I am physically worn down by the effort of the constant fight with Hanna. Every single day that the girls have been in our home, I have had to deal with something: field a complaint or handle a mind game or deal with difficult behaviour; redecorate a room or take an unnecessary trip to casualty or sacrifice a family treat. All of which has created extra work, and all of which I have to document in the logs. And it's not just the physical workload. There's also the emotional stress of seeing my home and words on the internet surrounded by messages of hate, and the fact of having the whole character of my home changed, even down to its smell. The pungent aroma that arrived with Avril and Sky has never quite left. There is, literally and metaphorically, a bad smell in the air. There has been something out of the ordinary to deal with every single day. And it's all energy spent badly, diverted to the wrong things when it could have been put to so much good. It should have been spent helping the girls to become confident and get well. But that hasn't happened at all. Even the small steps of progress have been undone by Hanna's interference, because the emotional and physical health of her children doesn't seem to be one of her priorities.

Sometimes I think she would sacrifice them entirely, just to make her stand.

It's not just me. I have to factor in the knowledge that the other children also suffer in multiple, immeasurable ways: the time that is stolen away from them day in, day out; the general tension in the house; the secondary stress of living with two adults who aren't relaxed because they are watching their backs the whole time.

Hanna knows how to play mind games, and to play them very well. She invests an enormous amount of time in it – she must do, in order to come up with each new ruse. I suspect that she hasn't got much else to do. I don't get the impression she looked after the girls even when they were home with her, but now they have gone she will have even more hours available to her. I become more curious about her. I don't think Hanna has had a job. Perhaps not ever. From what I have managed to glean from Avril, I understand that Hanna fell pregnant with her while she was a student and dropped out of university to stay at home. Her objections to Avril going on the pill seem hypocritical with that knowledge.

But clearly, she is an intelligent woman. She must feel sad that she hasn't been able to use all that potential in the ways that she might first have imagined. She is stuck with a man in a wheelchair and daughters in a system that she despises. Keeping house and being a mother evidently weren't enough for her. In fact, I don't think she was investing any effort into doing those things. I know that they weren't going out of the house very much, if at all. Sky's reaction to a supermarket and the high street, and even the park, have been enough to tell me that. So what does she do all day?

In an effort to answer that question, I have begun to dig a little more deeply into Stone Ground, the organisation which purports to use technology to try to bring down the system. The more I dig, the more I discover that Hanna Hopfgarten and John Wiseman *are* Stone Ground. They are the driving force behind it. Though they evidently have some support and following, the content on the website is primarily generated between them. The hatred and the vitriol and the spite that they spew all comes from within. In some ways I understand their frustration and am sympathetic to the cause. I am not a fan of greed, and prefer to believe in a philosophy that shares wealth and opportunity amongst the many and not the few – but the way they go about their business is fanatical and dangerous, and not just to their targets. I'm not sure quite what 'success' or what impact at all they are having on capitalism in the country, but what they are doing is harmful to themselves and their daughters.

I keep checking my email to see if there is a reply from Charlie. I busy myself putting things away that have been left to dry on the drainer, before wandering into the sitting room, dishcloth in hand, to watch my sons and Lily on their devices. We have been strict about time limits, because that's what you do as a parent. But what if it's the parent who is the problem, and it's the supposedly responsible adult who is addicted to the device? I wonder if that is what has happened to Hanna and John. I already know that Hanna spends a great deal of time on her phone, and I have seen where that has led. The website has new content every few days, reporting on their next targets. They must be spending an awful lot of time at their computers. Not to mention the 'hacking' itself. Is that Hanna, or John? Whatever – the message going out to their children is a strange one: that through a screen, in 'the ether', is the way to validate your sense of self and create purpose and meaning in life. What must it be like to be defined in that way?

I check my email again. Still nothing. I'm aware of the irony in continually returning to a digital device when I am criticising Hanna and John for doing the same, but I can't help myself. I want a reply from Charlie, and I want to know more about Hanna and John.

There is little online about Hanna Hopfgarten, but much more about John Wiseman. So I do much more research into his background. I have to make some leaps, but with an academic profile it isn't too difficult to trace a career path for him. Maz has shared what little she has been able to discover with me, which helps my search. I become quite fascinated by him.

John Wiseman had once been a successful academic. *Very* successful, though all that is a long time in the past now. His subject was economics, and his specialism was in social economics: a branch of social science that focuses on the relationship between social behaviour and economic outcomes.

He appears to have written some important articles, which I try to read in order to glean more. Some are open access, and others I can acquire through my own university library. I don't get very far, though; I struggle to get through phrases like 'neoclassical microeconomics'. But his early work was all published in the US.

I discover, if it is indeed the same man – and I've made enough checks to be convinced that it is – that he was actually born in America. His father had been a small-town rabbi in Detroit – so he's Jewish. His mother had been a teacher, and he came from a family of six children. He was the second oldest in the family.

I feel sad to find out that the man now confined to a wheelchair had been a successful athlete in his youth, and played basketball to a high level.

The pictures that I find show him as tall and handsome, and he was evidently a bright young man because he studied at Stanford University, a highly selective institution. Although Stanford isn't technically a member of the 'Ivy League', it remains a very prestigious place to have studied, and is often ranked above many Ivy League colleges. It is certainly ranked among the best universities in the world in terms of academic publications. And John Wiseman was a big fish. His student research helped inform the divestment strategy of South Africa's apartheid regime; he was destined for big issues policy and influence.

He married a fellow Stanford student, named as Nancy Mullein, and they had two children quite quickly, but the marriage fell apart after six years. There was a little bit of scandal as she moved in with her female lover – this was in the early 1980s.

He seems to have taken the break-up quite badly, because there are a few minor indiscretions in its wake: he has a drink-driving record from that time, and was caught with a small amount of weed. It isn't clear what happened to the children from his first marriage, but he then seems to have moved to take a research job in New York. Again, he began to attain some academic notoriety over several years, and there are plenty more papers published during that period. His career was thriving when he took a job at a Cambridge college, moving to England aged 35.

Just as at Stanford and in New York, he was initially very successful – raising the research profile of the college and fulfilling all his teaching duties with what seems like a great deal of popularity and success.

Then the first of the major blemishes to his career: he became embroiled in an affair with a first-year undergraduate student from Denmark. I know this because there are newspaper reports about it where he is named. It was scandalous because there was an 18-year age gap between them. Her name was Freja, though. Not Hanna. She must have been quite something for him to risk his career over an undergraduate. Or perhaps he was flattered by the attention of a young girl. Who knows?

The affair was evidently well known among the student body, and even more so when Freja became pregnant with his child. Perhaps unsurprisingly, Freja's parents made a serious complaint of misconduct to the university, and they are also quoted as saying that Freja had previously experienced sexual abuse from a man back in Denmark who had also taken advantage of her. Poor kid. It was suspected by his colleagues that this was a foil to protect the family's reputation, but it destroyed John's.

According to Maz, John never met his child. Freja must have gone back to Denmark.

It doesn't look as though he was sacked directly, but it was enough for the university not to renew his contract. There is a short period of unemployment.

Now with his career in tatters, John Wiseman seems to have taken a teaching post in a northern polytechnic where no one knew him. Somehow the mud didn't stick enough to prevent him from working with students again – or perhaps the polytechnic was willing to overlook his misdemeanour in order to get someone of his calibre teaching there. I'm speculating. None of this is considered in the online hole that I'm rapidly disappearing down; it's my imagination doing its usual thing, trying to read between the lines and answer the unanswered questions.

John continued to pursue his research interest in socioeconomics and became more involved with politics. He joined a number of his students in setting up an underground political group that believed in anti-capitalist theorics – a forerunner or early incarnation of Stone Ground. At the same time new universities were investing heavily in international recruitment. A number of new students from Europe and Asia had joined his programme, and a few heard about the underground political group.

By this point he was in his early fifties, not having remarried, but having now fathered three children that he had nothing to do with.

History repeated itself.

His relationship with Freja wasn't a one-off. He seems to have had a penchant for his young, female undergraduates. I feel cross then at the institutions. Really, how was this allowed to happen?

Another young student managed to get him to look in her direction, and this is where Hanna appears in the story. Hanna Hopfgarten was a German student who was studying politics. She was originally from a small town near Munich, and, doing the maths, she must have fallen pregnant with John's child in the second year of her studies. It doesn't sound like Avril was planned.

I do another quick calculation. That must mean that John Wiseman's in his mid-sixties now. That's some age gap.

The underground group that Hanna and John led together had its own struggles as young bright things jostled for leadership. Hanna's name drops out for a while. Perhaps

Hanna was ignored by her fellow students, or wasn't taken seriously in the group as a mother-to-be. Now I'm projecting my own experiences on to this. John must have offered to support her, and agreed to her dropping out of university to live with him and raise their baby. He managed to keep his job, for a little while longer at least. Perhaps Hanna didn't have parents like Freja who would intervene on her behalf.

His academic career seems to have ended there. Certainly he published no more papers, as far as I can see. There is nothing with his name on it in the last 15 years or so.

And then the really nasty bit. John contracted multiple sclerosis, hence the wheelchair.

He was forced to retire early due to poor health, and there were rumours around the university that he drank too much. The story dribbles out. Apart from his work with Stone Ground, nothing. I fill in the gaps. How would a man with all that potential react to losing his academic status, his job, his health all at once? With bitterness, I have no doubt. I expect that Hanna was just as resentful. Stuck in a country that wasn't her own, with a partner with a terminal illness. That wasn't what she signed up for when she arrived as a hopeful young student to the UK. Part of me isn't surprised that she wasn't very good at motherhood. Probably harbouring her own resentments and regrets about not being able to finish her degree, and not living the life that had been promised to her. She must have felt as much of a failure as he did. It can't have been easy to watch her fellow students flourish while she and John eked out an impoverished and isolated existence. Hanna must have become pregnant again, with Sky this time.

And now, here we are.

Chapter Twenty-Five

At the weekend, Sky comes shopping with me again. Pottering around town I head into one of the big chemists, looking for 'Plum Beautiful', the same lipstick I have been wearing since I was 15. Over the years I've dabbled with shades of red and earthy browns but never felt that they were me. While I'm chatting away to myself, muttering about prices and wondering if it's time to try changing the colour again, I lose sight of Sky. I panic for a moment until I find her in the next aisle, holding an old-fashioned washbag: the sort I imagine a granny would pack for a weekend in Bournemouth. I watch the way she turns it over in her hands, examines it carefully, feels the fabric. I can tell that she wants it.

'What have you got there, Sky?' I say, wondering why on earth a six-year-old would pick up such an object amid all the other marvels in this shop.

'It's a washbag,' she explains patiently, as though I might not know what it is. 'I saw a lady on TV zip one up and put it into a suitcase. It has music that goes dee-da-da-da,' and she sings me a tune that I vaguely recognise. Something clicks; I think it's a daytime advert for Saga holidays. 'I've always wanted one.'

Well, I can't resist that, in spite of Charlie and the Pocket Money Factory.

'Tell you what, I'll get it for you,' I say, having a sudden brainwave. 'And why don't we see if we can find some other bits and pieces to go inside it?'

Her response is the wonderful Sky beam, the smile that lights up her face. She is delighted, and I marvel once more at how easily pleased she can be. I help her 'choose' carefully as we look at bath-time products to fill the bag. 'Yes, if you were packing a suitcase, you'd definitely need a flannel like this and a little travel towel like this. Which colour do you like best?'

She selects a bright turquoise one.

'And you'd need these tiny-sized products to put in there,' I say, heading to the travel section. 'Aren't these little bottles sweet?'

When we get home she's keen to use her new things. So we play a game where we pack up her little suitcase. I put on my best 'hotel manager' voice (well, it's a voice of some sort). 'If you'd just like to follow me through here, I'll show you to your room. And here's your en-suite bathroom, madam,' I say. 'I think you'll find everything you need here for your stay.'

She takes the flannel out and washes her face and hands so that she can use her new soap. It's not time to get ready for bed, but I'm not missing this opportunity. She dries them on her new turquoise towel.

When it does come to bedtime, she asks if she could wash her hair with her new shampoo and conditioner. She leans over the bath while I shower her hair. It is the first time she's done this. Thus far I've had to recreate the 'salon' every time I need to wash her hair. Wonderful for her, but more than a little tedious for me. She complains a little, but then it wouldn't be Sky if she didn't complain just a little. And I actually find it quite endearing.

The next night she asks to have a bath.

Take those wins, Louise. Take those wins.

Charlie has announced that he is coming to meet us at home.

Maz has said that she would like to be there. It's pretty unusual for both social workers to come to an update meeting, and my antennae begin to quiver. Something must be afoot. I hope that there will be progress from my email, an acknowledgement, at least, of our 'inability to meet Avril's needs'.

The girls have settled back down and there have been no more incidents since the night of hospital-gate.

Lloyd has helped me do the best we can to clear up Sky's room. I have gone over the Sharpie scribbles with a third coat of paint just this morning, as two weren't enough and the pen was still showing through. I threw the new rugs from IKEA away, as they were both ruined. The bedding also had to be thrown out and I've bleached most of the white furniture, which seems to have lightened the marks.

Sky *must* have had help from Avril to do this work. From a practical perspective I don't think Sky could have reached where some of the marks are, and the styles and weight of marks are different. I don't want to talk about it yet to Sky; it's still very raw for her, and I think in her heart of hearts she didn't want to do it. She was simply being loyal and compliant.

There is hope for Sky.

She has a conscience and doesn't want to do harm to the people that she's living with. I think she appreciates what we have done for her, and likes us as people. Avril is different. I think she has been brainwashed. She's lived with Hanna and John for much longer than Sky. It is a really awful thing to say

217

about a child, but there is nothing very much to like about her. I enjoyed our shopping trip, and I caught a glimpse of the child she might be that day. I'm pleased that she stood up to her mother over her right to birth control, but otherwise, there have been few redeeming features revealed in the month or so that she has been with us. Much of the time she doesn't seem to have a personality of her own at all. She lives for instructions from Hanna.

Sky, on the other hand, has millions of her own thoughts. She has turned into a chatterbox and talks about ideas all the time. She wants to know how things work and why things work. Peculiar things, sometimes, that I just haven't noticed. She asked me very earnestly the other day why the washing machine wasn't designed with the hole in the top so that water didn't fall out of the front. I didn't really have an answer, because when I stop to think about that old-fashioned design, which she can't have come across, it suddenly seems more sensible. She asks questions constantly, she tries things out, she has opinions – unlike Avril.

The more I think about Avril, the more I conclude that it just isn't typical for a teenager to be such a vessel of hatred and nothing else. When outside in the open she is always looking around her in rapid, scanning motions, one eye looking backwards over her shoulder. It makes me nervous just to watch her; it's as though she expects something or someone to jump out at her at any moment. It cannot be healthy to live that way.

If I reflect on being her age, I know that at that time I was full of my own thoughts. I grew up with neglect and abuse, but I didn't grow up in a cult. And I have to remember that when I think about Avril. Whatever Avril has become or is, it isn't her fault, but it is disturbing that she is unable to think for herself.

The children are at school, and I finish my emails and tidying just as the doorbell goes.

It's Maz to arrive first.

'How are you, Louise?' Her tone is warm and friendly.

'All right. Sky is settling back down. Let me show you.'

I take her upstairs and show her the progress that we have made in her room. She has already seen photographs of the damage when it happened. To my dismay, I notice that on the drying patches of paint on the floorboards I can still see Sharpie marks. They are much fainter, but a fourth coat will be needed.

'And you've documented it all in the logs?' Maz asks.

'Yep, in the logs that Hanna will get hold of, and so will the solicitors and judge.'

Maz puts a hand on my shoulder. 'Look, I'm not sure quite what Charlie's going to say when he gets here because the details haven't been shared with me yet, but I thought you should know that apparently Hanna has made another complaint. I just wanted to warn you.'

'Oh, great.'

We start to walk down the stairs.

'Do you have any idea what it might be?'

'I really don't. Charlie will share it with us when he comes, but there may have been a—' she pauses for a moment – 'a Development.'

She manages to capitalise 'development' in her delivery. Lloyd has evidently heard part of this exchange as he comes out from his study. 'Seriously. What is it this time?'

Maz shrugs and raises her eyes to the heavens.

We head into the kitchen just as the door goes again. I leave Lloyd in charge of the coffee machine and go to let Charlie in. He is friendly and cheerful as he comes in to sit down.

Once we all have a drink, I stir the spoon around my mug a few times, hoping that someone else will speak. I'm not good at not knowing. So when they don't, I blurt it out. 'Come on then, out with it. What are we supposed to have done this time?'

Charlie has the decency to look a little sheepish. 'Claire, my manager, whom you met the other week. She wants to take this complaint to the LADO.'

Lloyd lets out a low whistle.

LADO stands for the Local Authority Designated Officer, and while that might sound harmless enough, they are usually only brought in to deal with allegations at the serious end of the scale. When there has been an allegation of harm or criminal offence.

I can feel my hackles rising.

I look at Charlie, right in his eyes. 'Come on!'

From his folder he produces a number of photographs of Vincent, Jackson and Lily. In the first image, Jackson has his towel wrapped round his waist. He has come out of the shower and is going to his bedroom. The next one is Vincent in his pants running downstairs. The final one shows Lily in her room with the door open, getting dressed.

'So, Hanna has made a complaint about the indecent behaviour in your house. It states in the local authority handbook that adults and children should be dressed at all times, and they should wear dressing gowns when not dressed.'

'You are joking,' Lloyd says angrily. 'Tell me this is a joke.'

I've always thought that the expression 'hitting the roof' was odd, but I find out what it means now. I'm so angry that I can't speak.

'I'm not joking,' Charlie says. 'I have to do a full investigation and you have to rewrite your safeguarding policy.'

Maz starts to speak just as I find my voice.

I jump in and reach for the photographs. 'I want those images, thanks. I'm taking them straight to the police. I believe this is breaking several laws, don't you, Charlie?'

He looks pale and remains quiet.

'I want a meeting with Claire. Immediately. I want to know why she thinks this is okay.'

Maz, who hasn't yet had a chance to speak up, now intervenes.

'Charlie, think about it. I think you'll find that the local authority will be in hot water if you pursue this against the Allens. They haven't done anything wrong. Avril has behaved like a peeping Tom.'

'And I'll tell you what, Charlie,' I say, a thought suddenly occurring to me. 'If I find that Hanna has posted pictures of the children on the internet then I'll go mad.'

Lloyd is one step ahead of me and is already on his laptop looking at Hanna's Facebook page. Thankfully they aren't on there, at least not yet.

'But that doesn't mean to say that she hasn't posted them somewhere else, or that they won't appear here,' Lloyd says, reading my mind.

Maz turns to Charlie. 'It's not my job to tell you what to do, Charlie, but you might like to think about calling Claire and telling her that this is going nowhere. Probably worth letting her know that Louise is going to the police station.'

He swallows. 'Right.'

He gets up and walks out into the hall. We hear lots of ohs and okays and 'yes, yes I'll tell them' as he paces around.

Lloyd is still fuming, quite rightly.

But I'm confused. I'm wondering why Hanna hasn't factored in the legality of her latest enterprise: by setting Avril up in this way, she is actually endangering her daughter for taking inappropriate images of children, and more seriously, for sharing them. With all Hanna's knowledge of the law and her preoccupation with rights, why hasn't she realised that? And how did Claire miss it?

He comes back in and sits down at the kitchen table, where we are still seated, looking at him expectantly. But I'm certainly not ready for the words that come next.

'The situation has changed.' He clears his throat. 'John Wiseman, the girls' father, died last night.'

Chapter Twenty-Six

I'm ashamed of my next thought. The darker side of my personality considers how lucky Hanna is that I won't now go to the police and give her a taste of her own medicine. And I also can't follow up on the possibility of the girls' departure. How can I do that? It feels, bizarrely, as if Hanna has won.

My emotions quickly stabilise, and I realise how ridiculous that is. I start to gain a greater sense of perspective. My next thought is how this terrible news will be delivered to the girls. Technically, it should be Charlie's responsibility, but I already know that he is spineless, and what he says to me next absolutely confirms it.

'I don't really know the girls. I don't think it would be right coming from me. Can you tell them?'

I know it's the social worker's duty to impart news like this, because sadly, this isn't the first time that we have been in this situation.

Maz, though, looks at me as if to say, 'It would be better without him.'

I think she's probably right.

Charlie can't leave fast enough after that, which suits me just fine.

Maz stays. I repeat my thoughts about how odd it is that Claire didn't realise that the pictures themselves would incriminate Avril.

'It may not be that simple.' She coughs. 'Look, this is totally off the record, okay?'

Lloyd and I nod in unison. What on earth will be said next in this kitchen?

'Rumour has it that Hanna and John actually have a bit of a hold on Claire.'

'How?'

'This is all hearsay, of course. There is some suggestion of her own safeguarding irregularity. Her husband runs an independent fostering agency in the local area. There is an allegation that Claire might have been enabling children to be fostered by his agency. That amounts to a conflict of interest. Though it's only small, this agency has some safeguarding issues of its own, and she's the company secretary for his business, which all looks a bit dodgy. I don't know how culpable Claire is, but the point is that Hanna and John found all this out somehow. Hanna was apparently threatening Claire with exposure if she didn't help her attack you.'

'Bloody hell. I suppose that explains a few things. When did you hear about this, Maz?'

'I only found out in the last couple of days. There's an internal investigation, and my logs were requested. Claire was making some questionable decisions and pursuing complaints that were unfounded, or in this case actually illegal.'

'I don't know if I feel better or worse knowing that.'

'Feel better. Claire will be suspended later today and then probably dismissed, pending the final outcome of the inquiry. Whatever happens with the outcome of her case, you won't have to have anything more to do with her. I genuinely didn't know what Charlie was going to say today, but as soon as I saw those photographs I knew that it couldn't go any further. I'm sorry you've had to go through all this.'

I'm relieved to hear it, but of course the main concern now isn't Claire at all. It's what I will say to the girls when they get home and how they will deal with this new tragedy. Maz helps me with thinking about the approach to take and how to word things. She stays for another hot drink as we plan.

I spend the rest of the day rehearsing in my head over and over again how to break the news, constructing a mental draft of possibilities of different scripts, imagining exactly what I'm going to say when I tell the girls that their father is dead – and anticipating how they might respond. Planning it out in principle with Maz on paper is one thing, but doing it in real life is another thing altogether. I have no idea what their relationship has been like. I've done a lot of research about his life, which has made me form an opinion, but I've never met him or had any direct contact with him because everything came through Hanna. He seemed to be a relatively 'quiet' character, but perhaps that is just by comparison with Hanna – and of course, under any other circumstances I would have been very unlikely to have had that much contact with a birth parent anyway. I'm dealing with so many unknowns. I don't know, for example, how ill he was the last time the girls saw him, or whether his death is something they might even have considered.

Lloyd decides that it would be a good idea to take the other children out for their dinner to give me a couple of hours to tell the girls, and to give them some space to process the news and begin to grieve.

I needn't have bothered with all the preparation. They already know. Of course they do.

Sky runs in through the door and it's the first thing that she says.

'John is dead.'

For a six-year-old, she has extremely limited life experiences. I wonder if she has any real idea of what this means. Are these just words, devoid of sense? Is she processing what she's just said? It doesn't seem like it.

Avril drops her bag casually down on the floor in the hall and walks into the kitchen. Normally she goes straight to her room, so this is behaviour out of the ordinary. She opens the fridge door and takes the carton of orange juice from it. For all her faults, she hasn't helped herself to any food or drink like this as far as I know. She walks over to the cupboard which contains all the glasses, selects a large one and takes it down from the shelf. She pours herself a big drink and gulps it down. Her actions are precise and deliberate: tough, almost like a cowboy in the saloon bar of a western. She looks me straight in the eye as she pulls out a chair.

'Well. That's that, then.'

I sit down opposite her. Her expression is unreadable. I don't know what to do or say, but I don't want to interfere. I know myself that when I was young I didn't always have all the cue lines for the script that 'normal people', those who had a secure base and were loved in a healthy way, seemed to follow naturally. When something difficult happened the teacher, the social worker – or whoever – would say something like, 'it's okay to cry' or, 'it's okay to feel angry.' When you've been abused and neglected, emotions somehow mean different things.

She doesn't say anything else, so I get back up and busy myself for a few minutes.

'I'll be back in a minute. I'm not going far.'

I want to find the other children and tell them myself, but Sky has already done it. A sombre atmosphere has descended over the house. Lily looks sad. The boys look uncomfortable. I guess that hearing about the death of someone else's parent brings uncertain feelings. At any rate, they are all quiet.

Except for Sky, who is happy playing with the toys in the basket, acting out voices of characters and creating a fantasy play world. Is it her method of escape? Does she really know what's happened today? It's hard to tell. It's a bizarre scene.

We need comfort food. We forget the idea of Lloyd taking the others out to a restaurant for their dinner. Instead I make a big pasta bake full of carbohydrates and solace. All eat without complaint. It is followed by a big chocolate brownie for pudding, served warm with ice cream. Somehow, they all seem to be in good spirits. Avril doesn't leave the kitchen the second the meal is finished. I sense that she wants to be near us, near people. I feel that this is a good sign. I'm glad I can keep an eye on her and she isn't shut away in her room. We select a film to watch together. It's not as easy as it sounds to select something appropriate for this situation. Jackson suggests *E.T. the Extra-Terrestrial*. I think it's a good idea until I remember that ET just wants to go home – probably not the message we want to be focusing on tonight. So many Disney films involve the loss of a parent: *The Lion King* is a no go; *Finding Nemo*'s out; even *Ratatouille* and *Mulan* seem insensitive. I think of *Up* and then swerve well away: the old man's wife dies in the opening moments, and the old man befriends an awkward, unloved boy. Definitely not. In the end we land on *Cars*.

All the children get into their pyjamas, ready to watch it, and I pile up the cushions and blankets in the sitting room. I watch Sky and Avril carefully. On the surface they seem fine, but what exactly is 'fine' for the experiences they are going through? It's so hard to know.

The film ends, and we've had plenty of laughter. I always laugh when the truck says, 'He did *what* in his cup?' after the Car says he won the Piston Cup. I'm not sure the children find it as amusing as I do, but it's gentle and probably exactly what we all needed. Time's getting on, so it's bedtime – certainly for the younger ones. I start to pack them off. Avril seems to be hanging back a little, so I catch her at the door.

'Would you like to stay up and have a hot chocolate and watch a comedy?'

She nods.

We sit, mostly in silence, through a few episodes of *Friends*, but Avril's facial expressions acknowledge a joke from time to time.

'Time to turn in,' I say, eventually.

Avril hands me her phones. 'Would you mind looking after these tonight?'

I guess that she has the maturity to realise that her mum would now be even more emotional and needy. Avril isn't just dealing with her own grief – she's involved in managing her mother's. Perhaps she is, wisely, storing her energy.

'Of course.' I put my hand over hers as I take them. She allows it to rest there for a fraction of a second before pulling away.

I leave it a few moments before I go up to bed myself – long enough for Avril to get settled. I listen at her door as I go past. I don't hear any crying, not even a sniffle. Only the sound of music playing through her headphones. I check again when I get up in the night. Just that tinny sound.

Neither of the girls has shown any kind of emotional response to their father's passing. More than anyone, I know that there is no 'right' way to feel, but I am certain that Avril and Sky are going to need the emotional support that trained professionals can provide.

I'm up early the next morning, my first job to email Charlie and Maz with the suggestion that both children will need counselling and support.

Charlie sends a message back an hour or so later.

All in hand. A psychologist and a guardian from the courts will both visit the children. Even though John has died, Hanna still has to attend the court hearing for the girls as planned, so the guardian is part of that process. The psychologist will be with you at 9am, the guardian will be with you at 11am tomorrow. Please keep the girls off school.

It all feels a bit much. Multiple visits, on top of the news that their father is dead, and the impending court hearing.

How much is a child supposed to bear?

Chapter Twenty-Seven

The psychologist introduces herself as Miriam. Her eyes crease magnificently in the corners when she smiles, as though she does it a lot. She seems nice, and I warm to her immediately. Her hair hangs down in long white ringlets over an ankle-length black woollen dress tied with a belt. Big black boots complete her outfit. She makes me think of witches, but kindly ones – knowledgeable and wise, with all the right potions to hand.

Sky is happy to chat away about her feelings, though I'm not convinced she understands all of the conversations. She beams and nods at every question and babbles away, but there is no reaction from her about her father's death, other than more beaming and nodding. It's peculiar.

When it is Avril's turn, I leave the kitchen so that she can be alone with Miriam and not be inhibited by my presence. I sit for a while with Sky watching daytime TV, but we have hardly got going with *Going for Gold* when Avril slinks past the door off up to her bedroom. That didn't take long at all.

I leave Sky for a moment and head back to the kitchen, closing the door behind me.

'So, what do you think?'

'Well.' She gathers her ringlets and pulls them over one shoulder. 'Both girls have serious attachment issues, but react very differently. Sky doesn't understand that she could even have *had* a bond with her father. Avril is – in my opinion – depressed. She's confused about what she should be feeling, too.'

'Yes, we've had a strange few days. Avril, particularly, has been very matter-of-fact about what's happened.'

'There's a great deal of work to do there. Sky is that bit younger and that might make things easier. I'll make my recommendations to the court.'

I raise my eyebrows, expecting her to share more, but she is already putting her coat on – black and cloak-like, adding to her bewitching presence.

Next we greet the guardian from the courts.

I'm impressed by what she already knows. She has evidently read everything closely and seems well prepared. She also strikes me as nice.

Though she is very tall, which could be imposing, she carries her thin frame gently, calling to mind a giraffe. Her name is Jennifer and the first thing she asks is whether there is somewhere she can wash her hands.

'The last house I was in wasn't as clean as this,' she says, laughing.

I offer to make her a drink and she reaches into her bag.

'Yes, very kind. That would be lovely. Here, I've got my own mug. Better safe than sorry.'

I hold out one of my spotless mugs, not a tea stain in sight.

'Oh yes, that will do nicely.' She pops her own mug back into her bag.

Jennifer tells me unprompted that she is unmarried and has no children of her own while I make us coffee. Then we get on to the main subject.

'So, the mother – Hanna – as you probably already know, is fighting to get the girls back home.'

I make my concerned face.

'But because her partner has died and she is now grieving, this may not be on the table, regardless of other conditions at home.'

I switch to inquisitive, and she responds.

'I went to see the couple at their home a while ago, and I can say with some degree of certainty that the house is not fit for children. Actually, it's not suitable for any of them. Without seeing it for yourself it's difficult to credit, but John lived in his wheelchair almost in just one spot in the lounge. There was so much stuff on the floor that he was trapped. Piles of stuff everywhere meant that he couldn't really move more than a few inches. He was stuck in that spot. Might as well have been an armchair rather than a wheelchair. I think it would be fair to say that they were hoarders. You're familiar with the idea of hoarders?'

I nod, remembering a disturbing reality television programme I saw some months back on the subject.

'Well, whatever you're picturing, it was worse. I had to clamber over mountains of newspapers, magazines and cartons just to get through the front door. Beyond that it was deeply, deeply unhygienic. There were very few patches on the floor and up the stairs that weren't covered in stuff, and wherever you could see a patch of floor or carpet it had a mould beard growing across it. But I'm rambling on. How are the girls?'

She's been unexpectedly free with information, and I am less guarded as I update her on their time with us.

'It can't have been easy,' Jennifer sympathises. 'I've only met them twice before over the years. But what a home life they led. Like nothing you can imagine.'

'So how come it took so long to get them into care?'

'Ah, well. You've already had dealings with Hanna, so you may have some inkling. Hanna and John are informed, intelligent people, sorry – I should say that John *was*. They could play the system. Hanna was very good at keeping the social workers at bay. It was the new head teacher at the school who pieced it all together and compiled so much evidence that the local authority had to intervene.'

Even though I've been on the receiving end of Hanna's treatment myself, I'm still curious about how she got around the care system so effectively for so long. 'How exactly *did* Hanna play the system?'

'Oh, she had an answer for everything. She got Avril to school just on census day, enough to be counted, then when the Education Welfare Officer chased absence, she applied for home schooling – but we're pretty sure that not much of that was going on. She put them back in the state system whenever that was investigated or questioned, so that she always seemed to fall between two stools. She just knows what to do, as did he – like I said, they were very good at it.'

'So how did *you* get through to them? How did you manage to get in the house if they were sending everyone away?'

Jennifer thinks for a moment. 'I think I got in because Hanna and John thought that I would go away after I spoke to them.'

'Really?'

'I think both of them had lost any sense of reality; they didn't see what I saw.'

'And what else did you see?'

'You have to picture it. The mess, the hoarding. Stuff piled up everywhere. The stench.'

I wrinkle my nose, remembering. 'It was on the girls when they arrived. I still think it lingers in the house. I get a waft of it some days.'

'I'm sure.'

I remember Sky's amazement in the supermarket, looking across at all the aisles of food and goods, and her wonder at some of the products we had in the kitchen when they first arrived. 'Do you know where they got their food?'

'As far as I know, the girls went to the local convenience store a few streets away. I don't know if you know the area, but there is a small shop on the parade next to the laundrette and estate agents. There isn't anything else there. They were told to bring home food for Hanna and John and were given a couple of pounds to feed themselves, but with no education about how to do that. I think they just ate biscuits, bread, sweets and fizzy drinks.'

'That explains the girls' body shapes and the state of their teeth. They were both malnourished when they got here.'

'Yes, that doesn't surprise me.'

I try to imagine what it might have been like to live in a house like that for those girls, without even the outlet of going to school, or going anywhere apart from the local corner shop. I'd known that they must have limited life experience, but what Jennifer has described is not a life, merely an existence. 'What did the girls *do* all day?'

'They had cleared spaces on the floor to lie and sit, little pathways that wound through the house here and there. They watched television or films. Hanna and John watched a lot of films, but mainly they stayed on their laptops stalking people.'

'Ah yes. Trying to bring the state down. I've seen the website. And have personal experience of their methods.'

'So as well as watching TV, they played computer games. There was a lot of technology in that house. A neighbour reported that the girls had sat outside one day with broken hammers smashing up plates and cups and glasses. I guess there is nothing to eat off or drink from – which is probably why there were hundreds of discarded drinks bottles and food wrappers.'

It's a terrible story. The world that Jennifer has created is shocking. As ever, I wish I'd had a bit more of a picture of what their lives had been like instead of having to try and piece it all together. I wish I'd met Jennifer *before* they'd come to us.

She carries on. 'I guess they forgot what was okay. I suppose they didn't realise how they lived. It had become their normal – but I can honestly say it was one of the worst cases of serious mental health concerns I have ever encountered. Hanna and John lived to fight every day. They were at war with the world. The girls were not really nurtured at all, so they are certainly the victims of terrible neglect.'

'I wouldn't be surprised if they'd been physically abused, too. I've been on the receiving end of Hanna's temper, and when she was first with us Sky told me that her mother had hit her with her hairbrush.'

'It wouldn't surprise me. In that tiny cluttered house they must have wound each other up intensely. It wasn't just physically unhealthy, it was emotionally toxic. I'm not sure that the children have always been the priority.'

Or *ever* been the priority, I think.

Jennifer claps her hands together. 'Right. It's time to talk to them. Because I've met them before and know them, I'll chat to them together if that's all right with you.'

I call the girls in. Sky beams and says, 'Hello.'

Avril stands awkwardly, as though she has never been inside the kitchen before. Her bravado of helping herself to a drink and taking a seat a couple of days before has all disappeared. She is back under the hood. She must be feeling insecure.

I leave them to it and try to get on with some work in my studio. I'm both distracted and absorbed in the abstract works I'm creating. I can't help but feel sad for both girls and the way that they have been so badly affected in different ways. It is so clear how Avril has been almost entirely crushed under the hold of her mother. She is like the shell of a human being with no thoughts of her own. She's lost her father but has no way to process it. I don't think Sky can even have known that she was a child until she landed here with us. I've dealt with some sorry tales in my time as a foster carer, but this one is deeply unsettling.

Last night, because I was unable to sleep, I went back to bed with the *Story of Art* book. It's an illustrated book and I've had it since way back when I was a student. It was given to me by a friend from the course I was on who had two copies. We are still good friends, and though I have many art books these days, this is one I return to. I have been staring more and more at 'outsider art', maybe because of my strange wards. Outsider art is the name given to the art produced by children, psychiatric patients and prisoners who create works that sit outside conventional structures of art training and art production. I have been trying to 'unlearn' what I think I know and work intuitively. I produce some strange work today: it's inevitable that my preoccupations appear on the canvas, regardless of whether I want them to or not.

236

I don't know what's going to happen next.

Lloyd and I have discussed at length possibilities for our future with the girls. Our resolve over the difficulty of having Avril in the house remains. We feel that if we continue to look after both of them, we will also be virtually living with Hanna – everything that we have experienced with her already tells us that she will continue to make our lives difficult. We can't keep this going. It's demoralising and draining, and the time spent fighting off Hanna's strategy is taking precious time away from the other children.

We haven't been asked what we would like to do – by anyone, at any stage. In fact, my email explaining that things weren't working seems to have been completely ignored. The social workers seem to assume that we will simply keep them, whatever happens, however much damage is done to our own family along the way. The balance of priorities feels all wrong.

Consequently, when Jennifer finally calls me from the kitchen, I am relieved when she smiles, takes a deep breath and says, 'This is a highly unusual situation, as we both know. No one likes the idea in general terms, but in this case I wonder if this sibling duo should be split up?'

I hadn't thought that this was a possibility. Nor had I thought it would be suggested by one of the professionals.

'How and where would they go?'

'Well, that rather depends on you. Have you thought about looking after Sky?'

Now is the time to be honest. 'Yes. Yes we have. But I can't see it working long term with Avril. Her mum is too manipulative and, to be honest, we've had enough.'

Jennifer nods sympathetically and I continue. 'We don't feel safe. We don't feel safe in our own home, and that's an

237

unacceptable situation as far as I am concerned. And that's exactly what Hanna wants, isn't it?'

'Yes, of course it is. And in a way, that means she's getting her way. I know that and you know that. The subtlety of what she is doing is difficult to explain to anyone who isn't directly involved. Don't expect the others to get it.'

I reflect for a moment. I think they both look so much better: clean and well kept. In such contrast to when they first arrived. Sky has lost so much weight, and what sweet, engaging features she has now that we can see them. Avril's skin looks much better. I remember the reports from the dentist. I think that alone should be enough to keep these two in care.

'And Hanna has got herself a damn good solicitor who loves to win.'

'Yes, he's found himself a little niche representing dangerous parenting.'

I'm surprised by her remarks. I don't think I have had such a candid conversation with a 'professional' before. Or at least not for a long time. It feels quite refreshing.

The next thing she says shocks me utterly, though.

'I don't think Avril will live past 21.'

'What? Why?'

'I've seen children who have grown up in cults fall apart. And let's face it, that's what happened to these two. They've grown up in what is essentially a cult. The family has functioned – or rather not functioned – as an isolated group defined by its unusual philosophical beliefs, and mainstream ideas have been excluded from their education.'

I have thought this too, but never said it aloud.

She continues, 'It takes a big, strong personality to

survive something like that. Avril is not that person. She is frightened, and she's never challenged Hanna.'

'I know Sky is different.'

I've seen her in moments where she realises that there's something wrong with her behaviour. I've seen her remorse when she has been persuaded to act out a scenario that isn't her own – that first 'attack' and the Sharpie moment. I've seen her torn up because of the guilt she experiences afterwards. But how to explain all of this?

'She's a bright little cookie, in spite of her limited life experience. She has a quiet determination, and an impressive curiosity about the world.'

I think back again to our first 'hairdressing salon' moment.

'She really wants to succeed. She wants to find another way to live. I can imagine her doing well – and she is young enough.'

I pause, because Jennifer is right. I can't see any of that for Avril, who has no friends, no life and not much personality of her own. Even her relationship with Josh was very short-lived. Instead she acts as an automaton, a machine to do her mother's bidding. It's a dangerous situation. I can only see more depression and loneliness.

'Look, I'll make my recommendations to the court,' Jennifer says. 'If the judge and the social workers disagree with me, then so be it. But I just want to say well done for everything you've done.'

I realise that no one has said 'well done' up until now.

'And thank you,' she adds, 'for providing them with a home. They've at least had a taste of normality here.'

I laugh at that. 'Normal. What's that, then?'

Chapter Twenty-Eight

The court hearing is in a week's time.

Sky's weighing-in, which began as a weekly event, has now dropped to every two weeks – a good sign. She is losing about a pound a week, and it shows. Her fitness levels are up. She bounces happily on the trampoline and runs with the dogs. Vincent has been teaching her how to catch, and they have progressed to cricket. When she's outside in the open air with him she doesn't stop laughing. She looks better and better every day. Her hair is almost knot-free and I have, albeit without permission, managed to snip some of the more wild bits off. There are no more dreadlocks. Her skin looks great. She was a pale child with dark hair when she arrived, but now she has a glow to her skin and her hair is golden with blonde tips. She has large brown eyes, no longer sunken back into excess skin. Her mouth is just beginning to appear from bonny round cheeks to reveal a natural smile rather than the buried-eyes beam that she started with.

Each time we do something that I think is normal – like drive to the beach for fish and chips and a walk, or head to the woods where there are good trees to climb – she thinks it's an amazing thing. A holiday.

Avril comes out less with us, though she has at last made some friends at school. She even invited her new best friend, Connie, over for a sleepover. When I spoke to Connie's mum on the phone about arrangements, she sounded lovely.

'We've actually known Avril since primary school time – not well, obviously, because she was hardly there. A few of us have been worried about her over the years, but it's great to see her look happier and attend school regularly.'

Avril never looks happy to me; she is always sullen – but then she is a teenager amongst all this, and sometimes teenagers just don't smile.

As well as the sleepover, Avril has met up with friends in town at the weekend. Her hoodie is increasingly worn with the hood down. I know that it acts like a protective shield for her, and if she chooses to wear it up I know that she is having an off day and feeling insecure.

Last night I walked past her room and she was gaming, but had her mum on loudspeaker. Hanna was talking, but Avril wasn't giving the conversation her full attention. All I heard from Avril was the odd 'yeah' and 'mmm.' A kind of acknowledgement without reaction. For Avril, this is a major step in beginning to put the right order into her relationship with her mum.

But sadly, it isn't enough.

We know that Avril will still deliver problems and conduct actions under instruction from Hanna. These moments are dutiful acts born of loyalty – and maybe a little fear – but each event, each complaint, impacts our lives.

A reminder comes soon enough. The following Saturday, Avril gets up early and heads out for the day. I'm keen to encourage any kind of social interaction. We agree that she will be home by 7pm and she has money kept separately from her pocket money for the bus.

Just before seven, a text comes in.

Can you come and collect me?

I most certainly can't. I have some friends round for dinner.

We are just getting through the main course, the pudding is yet to be served, and I have already enjoyed a generous glass of wine, as has Lloyd. Neither of us was expecting to have to drive tonight. Not only do I not want to go and leave my guests – I shouldn't, because I might be over the limit.

Hanna also sends me a text. *Enjoying your meal?*

Avril must have told her that we have friends round.

Between them, they don't half know how to ruin an evening.

Avril sends another text. *The bus has broken down. I'm stranded.*

I make the necessary polite apologies to our dinner guests, and leave them chatting with Lloyd while I phone the bus company to check. Surely they are sending a replacement if there has been a breakdown?

There has been no such thing. Avril is also not where she promised to be. In fact, she is miles away, far further than we agreed – in another county more than an hour and a half's drive away – and nowhere near the school or where her friends are supposed to be. What has she been up to? I don't have time to worry about that now, because I need to sort out this problem.

You'll have to get another bus. I'll walk and meet you at the bus stop this end.

I wait for a reply. It comes from an unexpected quarter.

My heart sinks when my phone rings and I see the number. It's the out of hours desk at social services. Hanna must have contacted them.

'We've had a report from a parent that as a foster carer you are refusing to pick her daughter up?'

I try to explain, but he tells me that I have a duty of care and that I must go and collect her.

Our understanding friends make their excuses and depart as the situation develops.

'I can't drive anywhere because I've had a glass of wine.'

The cheeky bugger on the end of the line tells me in a condescending tone that 'foster carers shouldn't drink.'

Because I'm at the end of my tether, I make an unwise reply. 'It's *because* I'm a foster carer that I need a drink.'

He doesn't find it in the slightest bit amusing.

'I'm afraid it's your responsibility to arrange a taxi back.'

I have no choice. The taxi costs £120 (and of course the local authority refuse to reimburse it).

Hanna knows exactly what she's doing. Not only does she ruin my evening, she generates a costly expense – over half my weekly allowance for both children.

I'm barely over this little incident when we begin receiving a series of emails from Charlie asking for clarification on pocket money. Hanna has repeatedly claimed that we need to give Avril more. From my point of view, I feel that £12 per week for doing absolutely no chores or helping is pretty good – and just as last weekend, I give her extra for buses and lunch if she does go out. The allowances we are given as foster carers to cover things like this are tiny. Charlie, in a rare moment of insight, makes a good suggestion.

'From now on, keep a little book and each time you give Avril any money, any little extra for the bus or a treat, make her sign for it.'

I totally see how this may provide evidence to stop Hanna from saying that we don't give Avril enough money and I do it, but I feel resentful. I don't like having things imposed on my life and home because of Hanna. I know she is trying to get everything she can out of us, but we are giving so much already. I also have a suspicion that sometimes when Avril goes out, she meets up with Hanna. It wouldn't surprise me if they were together when Avril pulled her little escapade last weekend. I suspect that Avril gives Hanna money: our money. And that's just wrong. It's money intended for the children. I can't support another household on top of that.

In the build-up to the court hearing, there are further home visits from different professionals. Miriam and Jennifer both return, so there is another psychologist and another guardian visit. We also have an appointment for Avril with a solicitor who is working for her. She is old enough to have her say. This is an uncomfortable meeting because I overhear Avril recounting all the complaints that her mother has made, and I hear Avril endorsing them.

'It's a nightmare living here. Louise withholds money. She doesn't buy us what we need. She imposes unreasonable rules.'

It makes me angry all over again, in spite of myself, in spite of the fact that I know she's being manipulated to say these things. That's not even the kind of language a teenager would ordinarily choose to use: imposes, withholds. They're not words that Avril uses in everyday conversation.

What I hear in these moments that's so disturbing is a kind of primal enjoyment. Avril enjoys stirring things up. It gives her a sense of power. Yes, it's an act of loyalty, but she likes causing trouble for its own sake.

No matter how much things improve, I can never relax; I can never feel comfortable around Avril. We never quite know what's coming next. She might be recording what I'm saying or filming us through the window or sending images of our personal spaces and possessions to Hanna to post on Facebook. Sometimes it's horribly intrusive, sometimes it's deeply annoying. We've had the estate agents' details for our house on Facebook, along with the price and a comment from Hanna: *These people won't buy my daughter what she needs when they are meant to be caring for her.*

Avril spends a great deal of time talking about how much money we must have. She knows I have published a book and believes – or her mother does – that I have made millions. Clearly they don't know anything about publishing, but the rudeness is wearing me down.

I feel further resentment that my voice isn't heard. I hate the fact that the authorities don't seem to care. Their priority seems to be protecting themselves from Hanna. Her determination to get at them, and us, is limitless. It really feels as though we are living with the enemy.

One evening, as we are settling down to dinner, she instigates a new complaint.

We have had plenty of them in the past: not enough, too much, the wrong food, not from Harrods Food Hall brought to the door on the backs of wild hares.

Tonight I sense a new tack.

'This is disgusting. I'm not eating it.'

That's rude by anyone's standards, when a meal has been placed in front of you. I'm as patient as I can be.

'What's wrong with it?' I look at the homemade shepherd's pie and the different vegetables on offer.

'I've had it too often. This isn't a varied diet.'

I don't know when we last had shepherd's pie – perhaps two or three weeks ago. I put a great deal of effort into planning weekly menus that capture all the children's eating preferences. My birth children have learnt to eat what is put in front of them, but foster children come with so many hang-ups and disorders and control issues that I am well versed in attending to their needs. Often they simply have no idea about food and are gradually persuaded to try new things, as is the case with Sky.

I look at Avril and think back to my email to Charlie. Further evidence that we *aren't able to fully meet Avril's needs*. I don't think anyone could, but I quietly return to hoping that our comment to Charlie will be taken into account – especially after Jennifer's suggestion that they might be split. I honestly don't know how much longer I can take this.

After dinner the children disperse to rooms to play games or do homework. Avril doesn't have homework. There is no doubt that she finds school hard, and she has struggled with attending daily. Because she has missed so much over the years, and is so far behind the rest of her year group, we were called to a special meeting at the school a little while ago, where it was agreed that Avril should not have homework. Hanna stuck her oar in, of course, when she got wind of it, insisting that this was detracting from her child's education – which was rich, given how much she has already contributed to the interruption of that education. But in the end it was decided that Avril needs a special route through school, an education plan that is unique to her. She finds the core subjects – English, maths and science – particularly problematic.

In many ways I can relate to that. I missed so much school myself that some subjects saturated me with anxiety and failure. These are not the best set of emotions to enable learning. We have spent time with the Special Needs Coordinator identifying Avril's strengths, and with support from her teachers, we have designed a learning programme of subjects and activities that she enjoys. It is all done with the best intentions. I'm not happy about the amount of time that they seem to put Avril by herself in a room to learn maths through an online programme, because in some ways it just feels lazy. On the other hand, she isn't ready to do maths alongside her peers in a mainstream classroom – it's a foreign language to her. As with so many other areas, it's all about funding. There isn't enough money to pay for a member of staff to supervise her for these sessions, but the reality is that it becomes another window of opportunity for Hanna to have unsupervised access to Avril. It provides several hours in the week when they can be 'together' to do their plotting. The days when she has the maths programme coincide with the trickier days at home. Today is one of them.

Lloyd bursts into the kitchen. I've finished clearing away the debris from dinner and have moved on to folding up two days' worth of washing. Doing laundry for seven people means that if I miss a day, I feel as if I know what it would have been like to be Pauline Fowler in the *EastEnders* laundrette years, with all the folding and sorting.

'Listen! Do you hear that? What's going on?'

There are banging noises, followed by shouting and a dramatic clatter.

Lily comes running in next. Her face is shining, and she is breathless with the excitement.

'You've got to see this. It's Sky and Avril.'

I run up the stairs with Lloyd behind me and Lily following in tow.

Sky seems to be wrestling her big sister in the hallway outside of Sky's room. She is manic – absolutely out of control. The clatter was my plant pot, which is now lying in pieces. But worse is Sky's language, which is obscene. Avril is a 'Fucking C-you-next-Tuesday', and a range of variations on that theme.

Avril screams that Sky is 'a thieving little cow'.

We arrive just in time to see Sky push Avril against the wall and bash her head on the radiator. Avril slips down the radiator and is suddenly quiet.

I charge towards them both, utterly horrified, maternal instinct kicking in.

Jackson and Vincent also appear behind me, drawn from their rooms by the disturbance.

Lloyd helps me pull Avril gently up into a sitting position. I check her over to see if there is any obvious damage to her head, or anywhere else. There's no cut or bleeding that I can see, but that sound of her head against the radiator was sickening. I try to gauge whether or not we need another trip to casualty. Avril shakes her head when I ask the question, but bursts into tears.

'Lily, can you and the boys help Avril downstairs? Sit her down somewhere comfortable and give her a drink of water. I'll clear all this up.' What I'm really thinking is how to deal with Sky, and how to find out what on earth has happened to cause this.

Sky is white-faced and crying. It's a mess. But perhaps both girls will benefit from an opportunity to have a good cry.

'It's okay, Sky, she's going to be fine. I know you didn't mean to hurt her like that.'

But Sky is inconsolable. She is in a far worse state than her sister. She is barely able to get her words out, but between heaving, juddering sobs, she cries, 'I hate her. I hate Hanna.'

I look at the floor by Sky and see Avril's phone. The screen is cracked. It looks very much as if Sky has stood on it.

'What started it, Sky? Don't worry, you're not in trouble.'

'I found her sweets,' Sky admits, between the sobs and the shudders as she regulates her breathing again.

Eventually it all comes out: that Avril has been keeping her sweets and energy drinks in her room, tucked away in the old suitcase, and stashed in her bedside drawer. This is not news to me. In many ways it's quite normal for children and young people in care, especially those who've experienced neglect on the level that these two have, to hoard food. I did it myself as a child. Anything I could put by for later, I did. I remember hiding a Club biscuit, the one with the purple wrapper that might have had raisins or some other fruit in it, under my mattress. I didn't always get dinner. Withholding food was a regular punishment for whatever crime my adoptive mother deemed warranted it, which turned out to be just about any childlike behaviour at all. I got found out and was punished, which is why I think the memory of that wrapper remains.

I've been fully aware of Avril's stash and have simply chosen to say nothing. This is partly because I understand where the need comes from, but also because my suggestions for trying healthier options have sometimes struck home – especially so while Josh was in her life. She has been eating more fruit and drinking lots of water, taking a keener interest in her appearance. Her skin is looking so much better, and her hair is much thicker and shinier than it was when she first arrived.

'Oh,' I say. As though it is a great surprise. 'Oh dear.'

I know, of course, that young Sky has a talent for sniffing out sugar as effectively as a trained truffle dog out on a hunt.

'Did you take the sweets?'

Sky nods. 'Two bags of Haribo. And a green Monster drink,' she admits.

Sky on an energy drink is not a good idea. She's lively enough as it is. I'm not surprised she was ready to fight after all that lot.

She is a mess. Now that the sugar is burning out, she is left shaking and scared.

I give her a gentle squeeze on the arm.

'Best stay out of Avril's way for a bit.'

Downstairs, the children have organised themselves into a team resembling a paramedic outfit, so attentive are they to Avril's needs. I also discover that they are cheering her up with rude sculptures of bananas and apples.

As usual, I report the incident to Charlie and Maz, who both email back immediately, expressing their concern.

And I share that concern. I am deeply troubled by the new turn events have taken. Sky was pumped up on an energy drink and two bags of Haribo, but this is Sky making her feelings known, and those feelings are most definitely angry ones. That was fury I witnessed on the first-floor landing, a pent-up anger that found its release. I feel shaky myself. It could have been so much worse.

We get closer to the bottom of it later that evening, when Sky also confesses that Hanna has told her to sabotage an event I am speaking at in two days' time. Hanna actually encouraged one daughter to take the sweets from the other. What kind of message does that send?

Avril has evidently continued to do a good job of taking screenshots of my diary, though I have got even better at keeping it under lock and key. This event, though, has been in there for months. I am speaking to a mixed audience of government officials, teachers and academics about a project I started with a local charity to engage young people back into education using creativity – hearts and hands instead of academic learning. I'm convinced that creating joy and curiosity at any age is how we help enable people to engage with education.

I have strong views about equality for learning, and know personally that if you are affected by abuse or neglect or have a learning disability, or in my case all of the above, you can be disenfranchised from knowledge and jobs for life.

I don't believe that just because parents can afford to send their child to an expensive school, this means that their child is more intelligent. I know that many of the children who fall out of education are dealing with stuff that many of us could not begin to imagine.

I'm concerned for Avril on so many levels. She's been denied her education, and through her mother's anti-establishment views has been kept away from school. Because of the little I do know about Hanna's history, I'm well aware that she went through education to degree level, because that's how she first met John Wiseman. She dropped out because she fell pregnant with Avril, and I wonder how much of her anger towards the establishment is wound up in her own sense of failure and regret. Perhaps she has researched my project and knows my views. Who am I kidding? I know that she will have done that. And, for whatever self-interested reason – she will no doubt have a justification – she wants to sabotage the event. I wouldn't be surprised if she has already tried to put some sort of slur on the work. I'll be able to find out when I speak to the guests. I wouldn't put it past her to know the guest list already and to have already contacted the names on it, perhaps via email.

This case is so hard. Much of what Hanna is doing is illegal. There are regular, repeated attempts to defame me.

She does everything in her power to try to damage my reputation.

The local authority doesn't want to go down the route of criminal prosecution. They actively try to change the subject and don't listen to my concerns. If I were to consider pursuing Hanna, I'd have to pay for my own solicitor. That would cost me time and money that I don't have, whatever she might think. At any rate, she seems to enjoy knowing that she's having an impact. Whatever my feelings about the woman, she's clever. I have to give her that.

Sky, a six-year-old, has been asked to repeat her destructive behaviour from before and trash her room. Hanna has suggested that she use Sharpie pens once more to cover every inch of the room, the replaced furnishings and repainted furniture.

'That's why I broke the phone and pushed Avril.'

At her core, Sky is good. I feel that really deeply. She has a strength that Avril has not, perhaps because Avril has been with Hanna for longer and has received more brainwashing. Sky doesn't want to play ball. She's grappling with her own conscience. She doesn't want to do what Hanna says.

I admire her bravery.

I'm sure she doesn't fully understand what's going on, but she is desperately trying to reset her moral compass with an instinctive awareness, responding to her inner feelings about what's right and what's wrong.

I'm impressed.

Chapter Twenty-Nine

Before we know it, the court date is upon us. We are all aware of the cloud of uncertainty hanging over these girls' heads. The permutations and possibilities are many. Will they go home? Will they stay with us? Will they be moved on? Will they be separated? On paper I am fully aware that there is a substantial list of complaints against us, each designed to influence the judge and solicitors and paint an unflattering portrait: we are a bad influence and should not be looking after Hanna's children.

To give her her due, there is no doubt that Hanna is good – very good – at this level of planning and organisation. She has always been playing the long game, right from the start, and her skills of manipulation are remarkable.

I have a sinking feeling that we will be saying goodbye to the girls.

In truth there will be relief, certainly where Avril is concerned. I will miss Sky terribly, but I won't be so sad to say goodbye to her sister. As each day goes by, Avril wears her mother's mantle with greater purpose. She now seems to enjoy finding ways to hurt us and disrupt family life.

Days like this make you aware of how the lives of children in care rest on a knife edge. The decision of one judge on one day can set them on a course for the rest of their lives. I wonder if there should be more than just that one person making the decision. It's a big responsibility.

I also find it hard to reconcile the fact that, as the foster carers who spend all the time with children – and get to know them better than any other professional – we are not really included in the process in any meaningful way. My thoughts, my insights and my suggestions are not taken into account.

The girls go to school as usual. We get on with our day, and play no part in proceedings. I wait for the call from Charlie. And wait, and wait. And wait some more. In the end it comes much later in the day. It's gone five by the time he rings.

'Louise, I'm so sorry for taking so long. The judge just kept wanting to hear more evidence. Every time it seemed as if we were reaching the end, another question was asked. Everything just took much longer than we expected.'

There's nothing about his tone that says I need to worry, but suddenly I have a feeling that maybe we are in trouble for some reason – a feeling left over from my own experience of being in the care system, perhaps.

'It was quite heated at the end. Hanna had to be escorted out of the courtroom by the guardian. She was screaming revenge.'

'I can just imagine,' I say, and I really can, even without having physically met the woman.

'But the upshot is that the girls are *not* going back home to their mother, however much she protested.'

'So what *is* happening?' I'm forced to ask. He has this maddening way of talking without actually saying anything.

Finally he gets to the actual news. 'Avril and Sky are to be split up in order to, in the judge's words, "give Sky time to learn about her own identity and be free from the influence and harassment from Hanna". So there you are.'

It's the outcome I wanted, but I feel no satisfaction. I have never before wished for siblings to be separated. It isn't a good feeling, even though I know in my heart of hearts that the judge has made the right decision. 'Where will they go?'

'The judge has recommended a support programme for Avril which includes being placed in a special residential unit. It's a highly specialised place that doesn't have any access to technology – or at least doesn't allow it.'

'Wow. I didn't know such places existed – but it's what she needs.'

'She'll receive daily therapeutic support,' Charlie goes on, 'and she'll be educated on site by a specialist teacher. One to one. And you're right: it's exactly what she needs.'

'And Sky?' I swallow.

'Well, that depends on you, Louise. If it's okay with you, we'd like her to stay with you in the short term. Either until she is adopted – or until we've found a good long-term placement for her.'

I let out the breath I didn't know I was holding.

'Thank you. I feel very happy. I guess that means we're off the hook as far as all the complaints go, in that case?'

'Absolutely. The judge saw through all the complaints.' He pauses for a moment. 'She said all kinds of things about you, but it became so ridiculous that she kind of defeated her own arguments in the end.'

'Do I want to hear about it?'

'No, probably not,' he laughs. I'm warming to him. Slowly, slowly, but I'm warming to him.

At the front door the taxi pulls up just as Charlie hangs up.

When the girls come in, they already know the outcome.

'Hanna's told us,' Avril says. She's downcast. It can't be

easy for her, processing all this change. Not only is she losing her mother, but she's losing her sister as well. The gravity of their history and her situation is finally hitting home. She heads to her room to pack.

Does Sky understand the gravity of this though, truly? That's my concern. I hold her hand at the kitchen table.

'Do you understand what this means, Sky?'

She nods, but I'm not convinced.

'You're going to live apart from Avril for a while. That means that you two won't be together. And for the short to medium term—'

She looks blankly at me.

'I mean for the next few days, weeks, there will be no contact with mum.'

I have my very serious, very earnest voice on.

'And for those same few days, or weeks, you'll carry on living here with the rest of us.'

Sky jumps down from her chair with a lightness that just wouldn't have been possible when she first arrived. She performs a little twirl around the kitchen floor and her face breaks into one of its famous smiles.

'Wheeeeeee,' she squeals. 'I'm so happy.'

Chapter Thirty

I'd like to say that without the constant negative influence from Hanna and Avril, it is plain sailing for Sky in the next few weeks and months. In fact, though, things that weren't so apparent before, when I was busy firefighting the Hanna situation, seem to rise to the surface quite quickly. When both girls were with us it seemed as though it was just Avril who was mimicking her mother, but as time goes on we see elements of that manipulative behaviour in Sky, too.

First there is the emotional wrench of saying goodbye to Avril. She is moved to a special therapeutic unit and, for the first part of her time there at least, we aren't allowed to visit at all. Even though Avril isn't one for dramatic outpourings and displays of affection, the two girls hold on to each other for a long time when Charlie comes to collect Avril. A strategic part of the therapy that Avril will undergo is an initial 'digital detox', which means no phone contact, at least in the first instance. Both girls know that the parting will be for a good few weeks until Avril is fully settled. If all goes well, then she can stay at the unit until she is 16, but it doesn't sound much as though she wants to. In her letters to Sky, which arrive periodically in cramped handwriting, Avril laughs at the term 'therapeutic accommodation' and the idea that it is a 'secluded rural location'. Instead she sees it as *a ramshackle rented house in the middle of nowhere, the ends of the earth. Our phones were taken away from us as soon as we got here, and there is Wi-Fi but they keep the code hidden. It's worse than prison.*

I know she is a teenage girl and there will be some exaggeration here, but from her descriptions it does sound more like a detention centre than a therapy centre. It is an indictment on our system that we end up punishing children for what has happened to them in the past.

Perhaps it's a reaction to being parted from her big sister as well as her mother, on top of having the death of her father to deal with; perhaps it is simply that because Avril was such a handful that I didn't notice how difficult Sky's behaviour actually was – but things don't settle down as quickly as we hoped for Sky. I think that perhaps I've missed some of the warning signs in my construction of a version of events that paints Avril as the problem. Or perhaps with her sister gone, Sky picks up her mantle. Whatever the reason, we start to see even more sharply the myriad ways that her early life experiences – or lack of them – have had such a profound effect on her.

Sky goes from avoiding physical and emotional contact to wanting *all* my attention for herself. She literally beats off the other children – or the animals – if any of them need a fuss made of them. She now craves physical contact and affection.

It's so clear that Sky can't have grown up with much affection at all. But she has seen me offer it so freely to the other children that, having passed first through a stage of aversion and revulsion, followed by a period of staring and total fascination, the natural evolution is to a stage where she wants to receive it for herself.

And Sky, being Sky, isn't going to share me with anyone

else. It's as if she believes that I have a finite cup of love on offer, and she should be the only one to drink from it.

I can't deny that I find this difficult. My solution is to try to snatch moments of time with each of the other children when I can, offering interest and attention when Sky isn't present. As soon as we think we hear her coming along the corridor we spring apart, abandon a hug and pretend to be doing something less important than being together.

On the plus side, Sky's health improves further, and her weight loss approaches a stone. It is clear, though, that her relationship with food is a complex one. I suspect that she will always struggle to manage it. After all, she hasn't even begun to learn good habits until the last few months, and by six years old, so much is deeply ingrained. It isn't for nothing that we talk about the 'formative' years. She struggles to control her moods and emotions around food, and though we try to control her eating by providing the right kinds of food at home, she lacks the self-discipline that I know she will need to survive in later life.

At movie nights, we have to stop with 'sharing' bowls, because Sky doesn't seem to be able to restrict herself to what might be a fair share. Instead of crisps and dips I switch to rice cakes for a while, much to the disgust of the bigger children – but Sky still gorges on them, and it's no fun for any of us. An air of secrecy develops as the boys take to some surreptitious snacking, excluding Sky for her own benefit, but inadvertently creating a difficult atmosphere around the subject of food generally.

I know I need to do better, because I've seen it before in children who just can't stop eating. The health issues are terrifying on their own, but there can be associated effects in later life around other kinds of consumption: of drinks and drugs, for example. I fear for all children, like Sky, who haven't established the skills of self-control. I worry about what adult life will bring them when no one is there to look out for them. In Sky's case, her reluctance to eat healthily is matched by her reluctance to keep fit generally. In spite of early successes with the trampoline, we struggle to get her motivated to do other kinds of exercise and activity of any kind. She seems to suffer with a profound lethargy, which in the beginning I mistook for over-exertion, and often put down to the tiredness caused by those long taxi rides to school. It is much easier to sit and do nothing than to make the effort to move. Those early habits of confinement are hard to shake, whatever we try to do.

And we do try.

We work closely with Sky's school, whose head teacher kindly chooses to use some of the pupil premium grant money they have been awarded in order to buy Sky a decent bike. Publicly funded schools in England get extra funding from the government to help them improve the attainment of their 'disadvantaged' pupils, and Sky certainly counts as disadvantaged. Because children from disadvantaged backgrounds generally face extra challenges in reaching their potential at school and often don't perform as well as their peers, the pupil premium grant is designed to give schools some flexibility in how they improve the progress and exam results achieved by these groups of pupils. Sky has some profound physical needs and I think, initially, that this is an excellent use of the money. More recently some of the scope has been narrowed, and it will now only fund classroom-related activities. Funding for improving fitness and social skills is no longer included. No horse riding, pottery or art classes or bicycles. (Anything like that now has to come out of the tiny and rapidly diminishing fostering allowances.)

For a few days it works. We make a big deal about the arrival of the bike, and Vincent and Jackson promise that they will teach her how to ride it. There is a novelty value in having this shiny new possession – just show me the child who doesn't love a new bike. For a couple of times, it's fun to take it to the park when we walk the dogs. I change my route so that we can find smooth places for her to ride and, as long as there is no hill to negotiate, she enjoys it – but only ever for a short time. As soon as any kind of effort is involved, she gets off to push. And she isn't keen to push it very far, either: after a few yards she just abandons it by the path, and nothing I say or do can make her take responsibility for it. After a few goes, she is no longer interested in using it. The stabilisers never come off.

Perhaps, if we lived closer to the school so that she could use it to travel there rather than sitting in a taxi every day, it might have more impact. But, however much we try to encourage her, once the novelty of a bike has evaporated, she can't be induced to use the thing.

'Tell you what, if you ride your bike to the shops, you can buy some sweets', is about the only thing that will get her on it, and it doesn't take a genius to see the fundamental flaw of that particular approach.

A visit to the new trampoline park on the other side of town is an expensive failure. She likes the neon socks that are compulsory and cost nearly as much as the entrance fee, but after about two minutes of half-hearted plodding around the place she sits on the side, demanding a Coke because she's 'just so thirsty from all the effort'. It is a similar story at the soft play centre where she is more interested in the fact that they sell curly chips at the kiosk and have slush puppies in giant cups than she is in climbing through the adventure play. She takes no interest in the drop slide. I am running out of ideas. We've always been a family who enjoys an outdoor adventure, but Sky doesn't enjoy the outdoors generally, and I wonder if that comes of being so confined, of having spent so much time inside as a young child. Picnics, the beach, the woods, the playground – all the obvious places for recreation – just become a place to sit on the sidelines for Sky, watching the others play as if she is one of the grown-ups. Her lack of enthusiasm for what might be considered ordinary childhood pastimes is quite shocking. She is just so very unused to 'being' a child.

I wonder if she will always be a little on the sidelines of life. I wonder if she'll reach adulthood without ever really understanding what it means to be a child. So much is missing for Sky. The fact that she has never celebrated birthdays, or Christmas, means that she doesn't know how to handle them. It sounds a straightforward thing, but it becomes a big deal when she tries to attend parties for classmates and family friends. Things go wrong easily, often due to misunderstanding. I know that it hasn't been out of religious belief that these big celebrations were bypassed – more out of her parents' distraction and lack of awareness of the girls' needs – but it creates a giant hole in her understanding of the world that's really difficult to fill. She doesn't understand why it is only the birthday girl who should be blowing out the candles.

'But I was helping,' she wails when we have to relight the candles on Lily's birthday cake because Sky has blown them out *for* her. Endearing from a toddler perhaps, but distressing in someone of Sky's age.

And I see many sparks of what *might* be, because Sky has so many lovely, endearing qualities. She is sweet and kind and has moments when she is deeply empathetic. When we watch a film she is sad for the hero even before the sad bits come, her round mouth turning down as soon as peril threatens. I know that there is a good person in there.

But so much of her day-to-day existence is a struggle because of the giant gaps in her knowledge of how to 'be'. It isn't just with sharing and joining in, but managing her emotions more widely. Sometimes this is about manners and just not knowing the right thing to do. Sometimes it affects her behaviour to a point where she becomes violent towards other children, and to us.

It flares up quickly, triggered by the smallest thing. We invite the child of a family friend over to play with Sky. Katja is six as well, and they have met a few times before. Living so far from the school means that play dates are really tricky to organise with school friends, and tend to involve me sorting transport or taxis to cover the distances. In any case, Sky still doesn't seem to have that many friends, so I do my best to try to engineer some.

Even with someone she knows well, she has a tendency to just walk off and leave them alone. She has no sense of responsibility towards them, no idea of being the 'host', however much we try to show her. With her parents hardly leaving the house and the girls never socialising, never having ventured beyond the local newsagents to buy their food, it's hardly surprising that her awareness of social mores is so severely restricted. Often the easiest way to teach someone is to show them rather than tell them. I am conscious that Sky doesn't know Katja very well, so I find myself trying to initiate the 'play' between them, as though I am a child, too.

'How about a teddy bears' picnic in the garden?' I say, as though this is the most exciting thing anyone has ever thought of in the world of play dates.

Sky shrugs, Katja nods. We busy ourselves setting up the blankets and bringing some toys down from Sky's room. Katja does nothing more offensive than choose to move the wrong teddy. Before I have much chance to react, Sky has shoved Katja to the floor and is hitting her with a hard, plastic doll.

Even though they are the same age, Sky's size and weight mean that she can pack some force behind her punch. I have to have an awkward conversation with Katja's mother; it's lucky I know her well enough. I don't expect Sky will be invited for a return play date, though.

This kind of behaviour isn't a one-off, and, unsurprisingly, it gets Sky into a great deal of trouble – especially away from home when I'm not able to intervene. We are called to school a number of times following different incidents. Sky throws sand into the eyes of another child one day when they are playing in the sandpit. When, with the teacher present, we try to get to the bottom of it, it turns out that the other child 'took the blue bucket'.

I grow to find that long car journey to the school as tedious as Sky must, I seem to have to do it so often. I think of those pictures that I discovered on the wood under her bed, of one figure beating another, and wonder if that was once Sky's norm, a norm that she is simply perpetuating. Nothing we say seems to make a difference. She smiles, apologises, but it's almost as though that doesn't mean anything, because the next day the pattern will repeat.

If the other children have friends over to play with, it generally goes the other way. Sky will commandeer them and try to take over. Of course this annoys Lily or the boys and creates tension. Having friends over to play used to be an easy way for the children to be happily occupied, but now I find that I have to be ever-present during a play date, regardless of the age of the child – on hand to intervene in case something escalates.

It becomes increasingly obvious that Sky functions much more effectively when she is the 'only' child. In some ways I think that she needs that time and space to revisit parts of her childhood that have been so tragically neglected, to be the centre of attention for as much of the time as possible. And that causes a problem, precisely because I can't fulfil this need. With the rest of the family to think about, I find it increasingly hard to give her my full attention. The more I am not able to give it, the more she demands it in no uncertain terms.

'Louise, now!' with the emphasis on 'now', is her favourite refrain.

The other children, perhaps understandably, become resentful – and fights begin to break out among them with disturbing regularity.

And yet, there is never any 'side' to Sky. Disagreements are quickly forgotten. Though she has violent outbursts, it is always a lack of control rather than any malicious or calculated intent. It is almost as if she falls into some kind of weird trance. And because the triggers are so small, so slight, they are very unpredictable and therefore difficult to second-guess and prevent.

'It's as if she has been programmed to react at random intervals,' I say to Lloyd.

And while we might be able to see that there isn't any underlying malevolent intent, it can certainly seem that way to outsiders, and even to the 'insiders', my other children.

265

I watch them suffer repeatedly at the hands of Sky, and that is very hard. Our evenings become time spent refereeing rather than relaxing. Behaviour management is crucial in preventing explosions from Sky, and we walk a line of diplomacy that would impress the United Nations' peacekeepers. When Sky's aggression manifests itself physically, I find that on the odd occasion I have to restrain her. At these times I move from peacekeeper into WWF wrestler. My ring name might be Ultimate Child Wrangler. I hate these moments. The only thing that makes it bearable is that I can see in Sky's face and in her eyes that she doesn't intend any harm. She just doesn't understand relationships and the world around her and doesn't know how to navigate them effectively.

I hear via the grapevine – well, through the social worker, in fact – that Hanna is making huge leaps and bounds in moving her life on. Apparently she is no longer nearly as angry or difficult as she was when the girls were first taken away. From our point of view, she is finally sticking to the rules and has stopped the incessant contact via text message. With Avril out of the way, she no longer has a direct line into the house. I don't know what has happened to enable her to move from attack to acceptance. Perhaps in the aftermath of the death of her partner she has reassessed things – who knows? I smile to myself at the fact that she is 'moving on'. It's great for Hanna, of course, but what a legacy she has left for her daughters – and for those of us around them who have been left to mop up the mess that she and John created.

Because it is all such a mess for Sky. I know that life is confusing for her. Our home is nothing like the household she has come from, and she constantly has to adjust every aspect of her behaviour to our way of being. She can't establish appropriate boundaries. She has no examples, no modelling, nothing to call on when she needs it. It gets harder and harder for the rest of us to compensate for Sky's limited ability to self-regulate, but we keep trying.

Until the day comes when her behaviour becomes too dangerous to ignore.

Chapter Thirty-One

I am driving home from the big supermarket with Vincent in the front and Sky sitting in the back. Sky never misses the opportunity for shopping; she still loves the bright lights of the supermarket and all the goodies that it has to offer. Today those goodies include a box of cream cakes. I have bought one each for everyone in the family and we'll enjoy a little moment together before Lloyd heads off on another business trip for a few days. I've picked them up because even Lloyd will enjoy the luxury of a fresh cream cake, and he doesn't share the sweet tooth to the same extent that the rest of us do.

'But I want mine now,' Sky whines from the back of the car. It is the echo of a long chorus that has been repeating since before we made it through the checkout.

'No, Sky,' I say. My tone is firm, but also weary. This is the billionth time I seem to have said the word this morning. 'I've already explained that this is a special treat for all of us to share together, later.'

And it isn't only because this has been designated as something for all of us at home – in truth, it's also for the very mundane reason that I don't want cream everywhere. Sky has so little domestic awareness that she is truly blind to any kind of mess. While I'm not precious about the house, things have deteriorated all over the place since Sky moved in. Crumbs appear in the strangest of places, alongside smeared fingermarks of substances that it is often easier not to investigate too closely. I know that she will wipe cream on the seats and get it all over the upholstery. Although I'm even less precious about the car than I am about the house, I just don't fancy the unnecessary extra cleaning today. And trails of fresh cream left to go rancid in a hot car isn't my favourite aroma.

Nevertheless, Sky wants to have her cake and eat it.

And, as is her way, she won't take no for an answer.

We aren't far from home, but I settle in for it to feel like a long car ride and brace myself to just ignore the constant pleas from the back seat.

So I'm not concentrating as much as I should be when, mid gear change, her hand shoots forward to grab at her cake. The box is nestling near the top of my shopping bag in the passenger side at Vincent's feet. I veer off the road and on to the side. The movement is instinctive. Luckily there is a soft verge and no pedestrians on this rural stretch.

I've been here before with another foster child, Abby, and it ended up causing quite a serious accident. The memory of that episode rises up inside me like bile. I don't want to go there again. Because I am panicking and overwhelmed by the fearful memory of the accident and feel pumped full of adrenaline from veering off the road, I do a thing I don't often do: I shout at Sky.

'SKY! You could have killed us. What on earth do you think you were doing?'

She responds by calling me an effing bitch, and more.

Don't get me wrong. I have heard plenty of children swear in my time. I have been on the receiving end of a few streams of invectives during teenage rants. And it isn't always the older foster children. I looked after a little girl once who

269

looked like an angel. Then one day she called Dotty, my little pooch, a 'C-you-next-Tuesday'. I was a bit shocked at that, to be fair. And this is on a par.

But more than that, just as back then, I am saddened by what comes out of Sky's mouth in the car. Children only learn these words and the anger associated with them from their adults. I began to get a different insight into what must have been happening around Sky.

I feel so conflicted by the time we have all calmed down and I turn the engine back on to restart the car.

When we do reach home safely, to share the cakes in a little goodbye tea party before waving Lloyd off, the cream in mine tastes sour.

Chapter Thirty-Two

It gets even worse when Charlie arrives in the late afternoon for his regular statutory visit. As usual, he spends some time with Sky first, before we convene for an update. I'm ready to launch into what happened on the way home from the supermarket this morning, but before I have a chance to, he begins to reel off a list of all the horrible things I have supposedly done since he last came to the house. He has his head down, fixed firmly on the page in front of him, refusing to look me in the eye as he rattles through the catalogue of my misdemeanours. I starve her. I lock her up in her room and don't allow her downstairs. I don't listen when she's ill. I stop her from seeing her friends.

'But she hasn't got any friends,' I can't help but retaliate. 'We do our best to organise play dates, but the school's so far away, and you know what happened the last time, with Katya.'

Charlie nods, though he still doesn't look at me. 'She also says that you shout at her. That this morning you screamed at her in a rage just because she wanted a cream cake.'

The horror spreads through my body. I can defend myself against the other things, but today, for the first time, that last part at least is true – I did shout at her. But, but, but. But I know that I will now sound defensive if I try to explain all the context to Charlie.

'She says that Vincent was in the car when it happened.

That he can back her up. You went mad and screeched off the side of the road. She says that she was very polite.'

I have a violent sense of déjà vu after our experiences with Hanna and Avril.

I remember Sky's 'screaming banshee' performance on the night when she whipped herself up into a state and screamed and yelled as though she was being attacked – even though no one was near her – throwing herself around the top of the landing like a championship WWF wrestler in a big bout.

Only there was no opponent – or at least I didn't think there was.

Back then I thought Sky was under Avril's influence, but after all that Charlie's just declared, I'm not sure any more.

'Look, none of this is true,' I say. 'She could have caused an accident this morning reaching into the front for her bloody cake. Do you remember the first night we met? After Sky accused us of attacking her? How unfounded all that was?'

Fortunately, Charlie has not forgotten that night either. 'I know that, Louise. I know you're a good foster carer. But just knowing it doesn't have any influence over an allegation. An allegation is an allegation, and rightly has to be investigated as such. I have no doubt that it will all be all right in the end; we both know that. But I'm not doing my duty if I don't investigate.'

Why isn't Lloyd here? I just can't face another investigation, and I'm so confused about what's actually going on here. As a foster carer I've experienced all sorts of abusive behaviour from children in my time, but as I say often, I firmly believe in the adage that all behaviour is communication. When children behave 'badly', they are talking to me. Sky's behaviour in the car was about attention, asserting her rights.

Or was it?

I begin to wonder if children are capable of gaslighting adults. Gaslighting, the action of manipulating someone through psychological means in ways that make them question their own sanity, is the preserve of domestic abuse cases, abusive spouses or intimate partners, and plot lines in *The Archers*. It *can't* be happening in my house, can it? Gaslighters rewrite histories so that the victim wonders whether such and such a thing happened the way they remembered it, or the way that the gaslighter says it did. They question their own thoughts, their own memories. A six-year-old can't have the capacity do this. They just can't.

It's considered a form of emotional abuse because it results in the victim's loss of a sense of identity and self-worth. I certainly feel rubbish. I'm doubting my own version of events. I'm reworking some of the things that happened when Avril was still with us, too – when Sky seemed to be the innocent victim. With a different lens, she could be the perpetrator. Perhaps children as young as Sky might be able to do this. Especially if they have such a master teacher as Hanna.

Because I *did* shout at her in the car this morning, this latest round of allegations sounds all too plausible. Just as I did around Avril in the days when I felt that the household was under constant surveillance, I begin to feel uneasy around Sky.

It's an odd time. The way that I begin to tiptoe around her becomes faintly ridiculous – but it seems the only way to avoid Sky's awkwardness and the sudden flares in temper that cause so much disruption.

Once again, I feel entirely out of control in my own house.

When Lloyd returns, I tell him my fear that it might all be too much to deal with, to live with. 'I don't feel safe around her.'

Lloyd agrees with me. 'We aren't meeting her needs in a whole host of ways.'

We reason that Sky needs to go to another, more suitable placement: an environment in which she can stabilise.

I've never met a social worker, or their manager, who has been happy about giving notice. Perhaps that's not surprising, because there's no doubt that it generates further work for them. For a start, a new foster placement must be found and, in today's crisis of shortages, that is always going to be daunting.

For my own part, I know that Sky could end up just about anywhere, with anyone, so it's a deeply stressful decision on all sides.

At the same time, it isn't acceptable that one child should dominate our home in the way that Sky does; nor can the needs of our other children be sacrificed. They need the right amount of attention too.

I hate the saying 'It is with a heavy heart that...' It's the sort of hollow string of words that heads of HR departments use when they make a team redundant, usually because they are making savings and attempting to look good in front of the senior management. But in this case, my heart really *is* heavy.

I love little Sky and we have come so far, but I can see that she needs more than we are able to offer her. In an ideal world she'd be in a placement where she is the only child – or perhaps the youngest with much older children around her. I'm not sure quite *what* she needs, but I know that, just as after making the decision with Avril, I sleep far easier once the decision is made. And that confirms to me that it is, indeed, the right decision – for all of us.

Chapter Thirty-Three

In the event, Sky stays with us for a further four months after we give what should be 28 days' notice.

With Charlie and Maz, and with the support of the other children, who become more tolerant once they know that an end to Sky's stay is in sight, we agree that it's important to find the right placement. We need to know that Sky is safe, with the right person or family. Given the nature of our own experiences, we collectively understand that this is crucial.

It gives us additional time to work hard on helping Sky to understand that she is moving on and that we can be part of that process in a positive way. I don't want her to feel rejected.

Our flexibility also gives the placements team time to find the right place.

Eventually, and in spite of many dark nights of doubt when I wonder if we'll ever find someone willing to take Sky on, a placement does turn up.

Charlie shares the details with me.

'This isn't standard practice, Louise,' he winks.

I wouldn't have thought he was even capable of a wink when I first met him, but I was wrong about Charlie. Some social workers and their managers use 'data protection' like a weapon to keep information from us.

'But on this occasion, because you've worked so closely with us and have extended the placement long after the 28 day notice period, I've gained permission from the potential foster carer to give you her contact details. In fact, she'd like to go one better and meet up with you.'

Davina is an experienced foster carer who has come through an agency. She's a divorcee with two older daughters and a son, all of whom have flown the nest, though the youngest is still at university. She lives on a smallholding not a million miles from us.

'An agency, though. That'll cost the local authority a lot more money than using in-house carers would have done,' I can't help but say.

Charlie gives me a warning look. Naturally, he's defensive about the organisation he works for. 'Well, with there being such a shortage of good carers anyway, and with the complexity of Sky's situation in particular, I like to think that securing the right home – rather than the cheapest one – becomes paramount.'

'It's good, it's good. I'm just surprised, that's all.'

'So, will you meet her?'

'Of course I will. Leave it to me.'

I already like this woman's approach, because it's the sort of thing I'd do. I welcome Davina's request and invite her over, after an hour-long phone chat. I don't sugar-coat any of what's happened in that conversation, and it doesn't put her off. She doesn't seem fazed by Sky's behaviour. She seems to totally get why I need Sky to live in a different home.

'Believe me, you can feel like a failure or like the worst person on earth when you give notice on a placement,' I say.

'I know. But it's about making the right decision for the majority, isn't it? For your other children. Foster carers' priorities *are* the children: whatever else happens, they come first.'

Somehow Davina manages to alleviate all my guilt. I'm already well disposed towards her, but I like her even more the moment I meet her. There's something very down to earth about her – always one of my favourite personality traits in people, and one that I tend to associate with the best foster carers.

The best bit about it all as far as Sky is concerned is that where Davina lives on her smallholding, she has a pony.

My relationship with Davina enables a smooth transition for Sky, but also for our family to stay close to her. Once the dust has settled on the move, Sky comes back to us for visits and sleepovers. I'm only too happy for us to continue the relationship in this way. My birth children can stay with their uncles or visit their grandparents. Sky doesn't have this option, so we become like the aunt and uncle she doesn't have. It's a kind of unofficial respite for Davina, too. As I know only too well, it's the foster carer who needs a break from the child every now and then, especially if the child's behaviour is as challenging as Sky's is.

There's sometimes a marked reluctance from social workers and their managers to see respite as important. I'm not sure why. In my experience it's a strong, powerful way of resolving potential placement breakdown issues. In the long term I think it would be cheaper and more effective to make this a regular part of the care plan – rather than moving a child on to another placement, to potentially face more punitive rejection. It might also limit the necessity for some therapies, certainly those that come too late or are inappropriate. They often come at a huge cost, if at all, and perhaps some timely respite might be all that each party needs.

To organise respite, we have to go through the social workers. This can turn into a war between departments: the supervising social workers versus the child's social workers, for example. While people are busy getting upperty-pufferty about who makes the decision and who pays for what, the child's needs may once again be overlooked.

Official respite can cost £30 per night. This figure has always made me laugh, because that only works out as a viable option financially if you don't actually go out and do anything with the child. This covers clean linen and a night in, but only if you feed them baked beans. Factor in bowling or cinema, or a pizza and sweets, and suddenly respite foster carers are working for free. So to not tell them, to have these reciprocal arrangements with fellow foster carers, makes little difference financially. Which is all a roundabout way of saying that sometimes Davina and I just organise it between ourselves, without telling the powers that be. So many foster carers, like me, roll their eyes at petty procedures, and work round the bureaucracy from time to time without troubling the social workers. After all, they have enough to do, and so often it becomes more trouble than it's worth.

Davina works hard at trying to motivate Sky to do things – and though she doesn't get any further with the bicycle than I did, she has begun riding lessons and likes caring for the pony.

There's a further glimmer of hope in a telephone conversation I have with Davina, too. 'Suddenly she's washing without being chased and tidying her bomb site of a bedroom,' are Davina's words.

'What's brought that on?'

'Sky likes a boy at school. She's gone all gooey and can't stop talking about him.'

'Ah. I see.'

And while I'm the last person to suggest changing anything for a man, perhaps I'll make an exception in Sky's case.

Let's hope she can keep it going.

Hanna

Hanna sits on a few inches of what used to be her sofa. She notices, as if for the first time, the stuff everywhere in the room. She becomes aware of her own smell: the pungent aroma of her sweat. She looks across the room and sees piles of rubbish – and John's old wheelchair. The windows out on to the world are smeared and sweaty. Just the way she feels herself, in fact.

She doesn't know quite how she has ended up here. Or what to do about it. Once upon a time she lived in a nice, clean, middle-class home. She remembers the smells of her mother's laundry and how her mother used to leave the back door open every morning, even in the winter, to let in the fresh air. She hears her mother explaining how to air her bed, and how she must never fold damp clothes.

She stands up and moves towards a greasy window, opening it as wide as it will go. She realises, in the business of that action, that she's never opened a window in this house before. She moves around the house opening all the windows. Stretching across piles of papers, broken furniture, filth, she opens every single one. In the kitchen she opens the back door and feels the air across her face. The air moves around the house, chasing out all the bad smells and memories.

She wheels John's wheelchair out into the back garden. Its emptiness is a comfort rather than a sadness. She stoops to pick up some papers in a box. The words on them make no sense when she looks. Notes about different companies and their misdemeanours. What does it matter? She takes the box outside and places it in the back garden. There are hundreds more like it – and box files and folders. She begins to carry them all outside, carefully stacking them up one on top of the other as high as she can before they topple. She builds another stack, and another. As the afternoon wears on, she gathers momentum. Her energy seems to increase with the space that she clears, and she feels stronger with every bend and stoop.

She goes out to the corner shop, head held high, for plastic sacks when she runs out of boxes. Even that simple act feels liberating.

By the time she has almost cleared the debris from the kitchen and made a path into and through the sitting room, she realises that she's run out of garden to stow the rubbish.

In among the piles of papers, Hanna retrieves a letter from the Housing Association. She knows that they've been trying to get into the house for the last five years at least. She picks up her mobile and rings the number on the letter. With some of her old assurance, she asks for help.

'We can offer a complete clearance, if you're sure that's what you want.' The woman on the other end of the phone is kind and calm.

Hanna agrees that it is, indeed, what she wants. They arrange a lorry and some workers for a few days' time.

'Strike while the iron's hot, eh?'

Hanna swallows. These are big steps.

She keeps working, stacking rubbish into corners of each room. It's only in doing this that she notices that the girls would have had nothing, no space at all. Nowhere to be, nowhere to sit, nowhere to lie, to play, to do anything other than exist.

Suddenly her legs give way and she finds herself on the floor, landing in carpets of mould and rot and hair. Lots of hair – years of all their hair falling on to the floor.

She looks at her hands in disgust. She gets herself back up from the filthy floor and begins work on the bathroom. It hasn't been used in years. No one has washed in here for as long as she can remember. The sink and the bath are both dry and crusted. She must have bathed the children when they were babies, but she can't remember.

Downstairs, she reaches the small shower room by the back door that they sometimes used – if they removed the rubbish from it. A rush of anger – almost violent – washes over her as she empties the tiny shower room. Boxes of John's old papers, research that went nowhere, are all over the house. He was working on a hypothesis and research for 'Reducing Poverty in Sub-Saharan Africa.' She pulls all the papers out of the box and throws them everywhere, grunting and swearing, kicking the remaining debris into the kitchen.

'You fucking selfish bastard!' she screams. 'We were living in poverty! We were as poor as your fucking research subjects!'

She stands with her hand on the side of the door to the shower booth, breathing fast. She kicks everything out of the shower, then strips off all her clothes and throws them on the floor, along with the papers. Her genderless, style-less clothes: his clothes. She has been wearing his clothes, and it has never even occurred to her before.

A small piece of soap is stuck to the floor of the shower along with more dust, more fluff and hair – so much hair. When she turns the shower on, it takes a few seconds before it groans and sputters into life. She stands beneath it. She bends over and reaches for the tiny piece of soap, itself encrusted in dirt. She begins to lather it across her bony body. Standing still under the water – hot, clear, clean water – she realises that scrubbing at her skin feels good. She washes John away, over and over and over again. A draught blows through the house. The cold air adds to her determination and her need for change, her need to get her life back on track, her need to begin to live again.

The Housing Association come, as promised, two days later, with a big flatbed truck. Three men help Hanna to load up nearly the entire contents of the house. A letter arrives from the solicitors who dealt with John's estate. She laughs at that description. 'Estate!' she says out loud, with contempt. 'More like a bloody state.'

But to her surprise, Hanna reads that she is entitled to John's university pension, as she had been living with him for 15 years. It comes as something of a surprise to learn that John has quietly planned for her and the girls. In a bank account that she knew nothing about, he has saved several thousand pounds.

She decides that she will clear the house and visit the famous IKEA shop (that she previously tried to hack, because Stone Ground had 'intelligence' that the original owner had dealings with Nazi Germany and slave trades in Africa). It was difficult to get over the irony that she has been slave to Stone Ground, and to a cause originally devised by John and a few fellow academics whose views were from the 1970s.

She hadn't even been born then.

It hits her that she's hardly thought about the girls in the last few days since she began clearing the house. She isn't sure if that is a good or bad thing.

Finally, in that moment, she resolves not to fight to get them back. She knows that they're better off.

Epilogue
Five years later

I'm working away in my studio when the doorbell goes. Thinking it's a delivery for one of the children (since they seem to buy more than the adults in this house), I open the door to find Avril standing there on the doorstep – with another girl, whom she introduces as Suzy. I'm ashamed to say that, for a moment, I recoil slightly, even after all this time. My first instinct is to assume that she is here for some spiteful reason. Her face breaks into a smile that reminds me of her sister's beaming face. I'm astonished that she's here, but it turns into a joyful afternoon and evening. I'm struck by Avril's wisdom and maturity as she talks about the intervening years and speaks about her plans, reflecting on the child she once was, and all the trouble she caused when she was here. She's in the second year of a law degree. She's keen to specialise in children's law and rights. Her long-term goal is to become a judge. Suzy, a fellow law undergraduate, is actually her partner, and they've been in a stable relationship since the first year of the course and have moved in together. I smile as I remember all the concern we had over Josh and how far their relationship was going, and getting Avril contraception. I'm glad she's found her way. Both Avril and Suzy are vegans and live a relatively disciplined life, shunning 'typical' student activities.

Both young women stay for dinner and the other children – and our latest foster children – gather round to hear their news. Vincent and Jackson remember Avril clearly, even though they were much younger. I sit in amazement for most of the evening, and I find that I can't stop smiling at this beautiful, intelligent young woman who has somehow got her life together, despite John and Hanna's behaviour, and all the negative influences she experienced. She relives her time at the therapeutic unit, and I discover that the letters she sent perhaps weren't quite the hyperbolic ramblings of an angry teenager. She had an awful time, and she's only too happy to tell us all about it.

There were three other residents alongside Avril.

'The other girls – let's call them Sam, Sal and Sadie,' she says, in a way that tells me that those were definitely not their real names. 'They were there because they were involved with gangs, and the supposed isolation of the unit was an attempt to cut them off from these gangs. The social workers and care home staff stupidly believed that taking our phones away would be enough to cut off communication. But we all had access to money and could take a bus into town, so we became like little escaping ninjas,' she laughs.

'And don't tell me, you managed to buy new phones and keep them hidden.'

'Of course we did. I was always resourceful, you know that.'

'And master of hiding a phone,' I say.

'So once we were in communication with the outside world, we worked out ways to become free to catch up with old friends, and some less savoury influences – though I did stay out of Hanna's way initially,' she says. 'And by the time I saw her again, she had begun to sort herself out.'

She tells us how the therapeutic unit wasn't being run properly – in fact the manager hardly appeared, and there was little therapy. The home was privately owned by a senior member of the management team at children's social care and two business partners. It was a world away from the marketing material that had been shared with all of us at the time.

'Those girls were victims of exploitation. Men from the gangs would meet them in the lane along from the house while the night staff were asleep.'

Avril explains how, contrary to the rules, staff in the unit would enjoy a glass or two of alcohol of an evening, believing their charges to be safe. As far as the authorities were concerned, the isolation of the house counted as sufficient protection. They didn't count on the ingenuity of the girls – nor the persistence of the gangs.

'So I phoned a local journalist to report the corruption and poor practice within the home.'

That doesn't surprise me either. She's a chip off the old block, and using the media would be second nature to Avril, given the environment she grew up in.

'I told them that one of the caregivers at the home supplied us with cannabis – which was true. The night staff was also mostly made up of men, and I wasn't comfortable with the way they went about things. Sal, Sarah and Sam had told me about the sexual abuse that they'd each suffered, so I knew it wasn't right that it was being managed like this. It was totally inappropriate. And Hanna had taught me nothing if not how to kick up a fuss.'

I don't correct the fact that she's already changed the names of her accomplices. I find it touching that she's protecting them.

'Early activism,' I say.

'Yes, I suppose. Fed by my friends' fear. I told the journalist how one of the male workers supplied us all with vodka one night. The other girls got drunk, along with the staff member. I played along too, but I was actually busy with the camera on my secret phone, filming the man and his antics. The material looked very compromising.'

'I'll bet it did.'

Avril makes a good storyteller. She tells us how she sent the footage to the journalist who, with damning photographic evidence of activities at the home and the potential of a big story, was now paying attention.

'But I also wasn't going to hang around the place for another night with that creep of a staff member. While they were all partying in the living room of the house, I broke into the office and photographed the confidential files that had been left out on the desk – files that detailed the lives of my three friends and documented their vulnerability.'

'Why? They were your friends.'

'It was more fuel for my newspaper contact. But I'm not proud of the next bit.'

She drops her voice as she confesses that she located a can of petrol, 'illegally stowed in one of the outbuildings,' and poured it over a staff member's car – before setting fire to it. It took only a few minutes for the blaze to take hold and for thick, black smoke to fill the air. She filmed this too, and sent the clip to the journalist.

Within minutes an ambulance, police and fire engines were moving at speed towards the home. Sirens lit up the night, along with the smoke signal she had created.

The supervisor for the home also arrived and managed to intercept Avril as she attempted to leave the property.

'Got you!'

'Get off me!'

'You're not going anywhere. The place is surrounded by police – thanks to your antics.'

'So? There are videos of your staff's "antics", so what are you going to do about that?'

'I'm going to make a deal with you. If you say nothing to the police or the other services about the home, you can take this money and walk away.'

He reached into his pocket and showed her a bundle of notes. 'There's £500 in cash. Take it or leave it.'

She took it and walked away from the scene.

The journalist arrived and reported his knowledge of the incident, showing Avril's messages to the police. The night worker and the manager were quickly arrested. Avril was picked up shortly afterwards, and thankfully moved on. She survived the next few years in the care system, always living by her wits. At 16 she was placed in a form of assisted living accommodation – which was also awful. She was placed in cheap housing – perhaps ironically, not far from where she'd lived with John and Hanna in Crickleborough. It was an unfortunate place. The kind of dwelling which, because it's cheap, nestles next to drug dealers and other individuals of dubious influence. Trouble shadowed her, or she found it, but her habit of documenting everything kept her from the severest of penalties. And eventually, she found her route out.

Because she fell within the care system, Avril's education was supported into university. A late starter in literacy and learning generally, she was finally able to flourish. She learnt to keep quiet about her history, finding that honesty about her background did her no favours socially. She got on with her studies, and her life. The experiences she had already been through meant that she felt older and wiser than her contemporaries, and that maturity shone through in her writing. She was already a master at finding evidence to support an argument, so essays came easily to her.

But this brush with the wrongness of everything made her want to put things right, and that's when she began taking her education more seriously, and started thinking about becoming a lawyer. Her natural wariness means that she has an innate ability to question and challenge everything, and she's very sharp – attributes that make her ideally suited to her chosen subject. She wants to acquire as much legal experience as possible, moving through the professional ranks.

'I think it also comes from a childhood filled with protests,' she reasons. 'There were times when I'd be involved in direct action with our parents, and the other times when I'd be left at home with Sky, who was a toddler then, for hours or sometimes days while John and Hanna were off campaigning or protesting. It was just what they did. What we did.'

She remembers the Saffron Revolution that her parents were heavily involved with. Stone Ground had donated significant amounts of money to the Buddhist monks who were protesting against the Burmese national government. Avril has memories of strange men with no hair turning up at their house and having meetings with her father. In 2012 she was taken to Occupy London and camped outside St Paul's Cathedral until they were forcibly removed.

'As a lawyer I'll never support illegal protests, but there are legal ways to catch the media's attention,' she grins.

She tells me that her mother has found a new partner, Ruben, and 'sorted herself out'. Hanna had a bit of an epiphany after John died.

'She was only 19 when she had me. She was only 33 when John died. She missed out not just on her education and getting a degree, but on a chance of happiness. She spent most of her adult life with a man old enough to be her own father.' Avril's maturity is remarkable. 'I know she didn't do right by us, but I forgive her. Her youth was snatched away, too. With the money John left, she trained as an acupuncturist. It suits her. I go and stay with them occasionally, now that they've settled into a decent relationship.'

Avril and Suzy also talk earnestly about adopting children of their own one day, when they are fully qualified and their earnings and lifestyle allow.

I'm so pleased that things have worked out for Avril, and that she hasn't fulfilled that horrible prophecy of being dead by the age of 21. I had it wrong. Though she was in that toxic environment much longer than Sky, being the oldest – with the added responsibility that brings – it has given her a toughness that has helped her to survive. And not just to survive, but actually to thrive: to use her experience for good. Avril surprises everyone, no one more so than me.

I just hope that Sky can do the same.

Afterword

When I initially began to write *Sky's Story*, I found it too emotional and too demanding. I put it down, unable to get going. When I went back to it later, I still found the whole scenario to be, on some days, so strange and demoralising to revisit that I often felt too drained and upset to deal with it. The words were hard to get down on paper.

Her story wasn't like the others – like Stella or Abby, or Eden or Jacob, the first children that I wrote about in the Thrown Away Children series.

So much of what happened to Sky should not have happened. She didn't come from a situation of extreme poverty. Her parents were from the educated middle classes. They should have been well equipped to look after children – or that's what I thought. On paper they belonged to a world that was familiar to me: I worked in university settings for 20 years. In many ways, Sky's parents were like so many people I used to know from my teaching days at university. But, like many others, I made some wrong assumptions.

I think part of my difficulty in writing stemmed from feeling a little bit at sea – and perhaps a bit ashamed – because Sky's story messed with what I thought I knew about the world. I naively thought that on some level her parents were 'my people'. I wonder if, as a society, we are more shocked when the apparent middle-class intelligentsia buck our system and reveal themselves to be the authors of abuse and neglect of children, rather than the 'easier' assumption that it's the poor and uneducated who are responsible. Maybe the latter is a narrative that suits us more.

Either way, it remains a disturbing story.

So the difficulty in writing this story emerged not because of what happened to Sky and Avril, but because of the effect it had on me and my world. My preconceptions and my own values were all tested by Sky and her family. It's important to remember that when we foster or adopt a child, we then have to learn to live with not just the child, but their family and their ghosts.

I also suffered personally because of the peculiar form of 'gaslighting' that I experienced. I say 'peculiar' because it was from another woman – a mother – and not a partner. I felt ambushed by Hanna, under siege in my own home.

Now, let's think about that for a minute. What does our home mean to any of us? The standard answer might include reference to it being a place of safety. I hope that's true for most people who read this book. For many children, it is *not* a safe place. It's dangerous. I can personally vouch for that from my own abusive childhood experiences. But for most, home is a safe haven. Now imagine it under attack. The feeling I had was akin to the feeling that some people have if they are unlucky enough to be burgled. That vulnerability is often unexpected.

And that was how I felt: vulnerable. To have the kind of accusations that Hanna was making endorsed by representatives of social services, albeit briefly, was another body blow. I felt that we didn't matter, and that my whole family had been unwittingly drawn into something damaging, when what we had been trying to do was help in order to meet the complex needs of the children in our care.

Those needs aren't just the immediate ones, but also the long-term ones.

We are preparing children so that in future life they can keep a job. They need to learn to be respectful to their future employer. They need to learn how to keep friendships, and to understand the efficacy around having friends. They have to find a way to love. Love, for a child who has not had positive emotional experiences, is complex. Being 'in love' may not be healthy. They may make, or receive, dependency, embarking on relationships that are manipulative and harmful.

This work is so important that as foster carers we simply must do all we can to make it happen: it's our duty. It wasn't happening with Avril when both girls were together, and then it wasn't happening with Sky when she was on her own. And, as a foster carer and parent, I need always to be realistic about what I can provide. Although I wanted to promise everything and save the world, the pragmatic view was that we couldn't offer the intensity of time and additional consideration that Sky needed, at the same time as caring properly for three other children. It wasn't fair on any of them, or on us – which is why we made the decision to give notice on the placement.

And Sky scared me. It's as simple as that. It wasn't just my fear about how she was, how she behaved, or what she looked like – but how she could be in the future: what all of that might turn into. She exposed all my own fears about the world, and reminded me how close any of us can get to 'cult-like' obsessions. My real fear was how dangerous she could become if she didn't move on and away from the early brainwashing that she had experienced.

The Stone Ground Group is a fictional organisation, but it is similar in set-up to one that the real-life Hanna and John belonged to. Stone Ground as a political organisation became the religion. Faith and hope for a different world drove their beliefs and actions. By the same token, Hanna was caught up in the cult of Stone Ground. She became obsessed with its mission and, for a time at least, didn't see the children in front of her. But she had focused so closely on this because she was clearly not happy in her own right.

Unexpectedly, I found a good friend in Davina, and we remain close. Like me, Davina is keen on the idea of self-regulation as the key to success and happiness for a child, and is therefore committed to supporting Sky to find a route towards it. Children who have coping mechanisms for stress, anger, disappointment and frustration are more able to do well in school, with friends, and at home. Davina and I both oppose using medication in the first instance, unlike some foster carers who want to. Medication might decrease challenging behaviour initially, but it won't teach children the skills they need to manage stress in the long term. It's much harder work to work with a child and teach them how to regulate than it is to rely on a medication to do the same job – but having each other on the other end of the phone helps.

Sky and Avril have seen less and less of each other as time goes on, but perhaps their relationship might blossom again one day in the future. That early shared history will be important one day, when Sky has caught up with Avril and found herself, when she knows who she really is. Perhaps Avril can become the role model that she never had. Their parents had such a powerful influence, it was essential that they had time and space to figure out what had happened and forge their own paths towards their future.

Sky, like Avril, is very quick-thinking, very sharp. She could have a wonderful future, but unlike her big sister (who, on reflection, perhaps did most of the work and caring for

Sky), she doesn't seem to have the drive and determination to get there.

I truly hope she finds it one day.

Meanwhile, the fostering system in which she functions needs some work.

I'm an experienced foster carer who has been in the fostering world for many years now. So much so that I am part of a scheme known as 'Fostering Plus'. This is a special scheme with a limited number of places reserved for what are considered to be the top 10 per cent of the most challenging and troubled children in the care system. Being part of Fostering Plus requires the foster carers to make a commitment to undertake additional and specific responsibilities or tasks to meet the needs of the child placed with them, including attendance at support groups and training as specified, and the provision of progress reports on the child as requested – some of what passes for 'normal' in my day-to-day experience of fostering, and parts of which I have referenced during *Sky's Story*. Because of the complexity of the cases categorised in this top 10 per cent, payment of an additional fee in addition to the fostering allowance is offered. Factor in the fact that these children with more complex needs are actually becoming the norm, and you have a situation that causes tension between foster carers who are on 30p per hour and those on 15p per hour for the same work. I'm one of the lucky ones, then, in the 'top' bracket – meaning that I receive the equivalent, currently, of 30p per hour to work and be available 24/7. And so, by agreeing to do this, in a way, I unwittingly subscribe to this cult of being 'good' for the sake of it, for the love of the children. I don't – and nor do any honest foster carers – love *all* the children. How could we? That would be impossible.

To me it's simple: have exceptional people who know and understand what to do, love their work, and do the work: and make their lives good. Prevent the opportunity for greed, and direct the money to the children instead. Stop the self-fulfilling prophecy of our young people ending up on the streets or in young offenders' prisons.

Change the ethos.